Edith Stein

Philosopher, Carmelite Nun, Holocaust Martyr

by Jean de Fabrégues

St. Paul Books & Media

Nihil Obstat:
   John A. Goodwine, JCD
   Censor Librorum
Imprimatur:
   Terence J. Cooke, VG
   New York, NY
   1965

Library of CongressCataloging-in-Publication Data

Fabrégues, Jean de.
   [Conversion d'Edith Stein, English]
   Edith Stein: philosopher, Carmelite nun, Holocaust martyr /
Jean de Fabrégues.
        p.   cm.
   ISBN 0-8198-2333-3
   1. Stein, Edith, 1891-1942.   2. Carmelite Nuns—Germany—
Biography.   3. Philosophers—Germany—Biography.   4. Converts,
Catholic—Germany—Biography.   5. Christian martyrs—
Germany—Biography.   I. Title.
BX4705.S814F313   1993
271'.97102—dc20
[B]   93-2771
                                                            CIP

The Scripture quotations contained herein are from the New Revised Standard Version Bible, copyrighted © 1989 by the Division of Christian Education of the National Council of Churches of Christ in the U.S.A., and are used by permission. All rights reserved.

Translated from the French by Donald M. Antoine

Original title: *La Conversion d'Edith Stein*, published by Wesmael-Charlier, Paris

Printed and published in the U.S.A. by St. Paul Books & Media, 50 St. Paul's Avenue, Boston, MA 02130.

St. Paul Books & Media is the publishing house of the Daughters of St. Paul, an international congregation of women religious serving the Church with the communications media.

        1 2 3 4 5 6 7 8 9   99 98 97 96 95 94 93

Contents

Preface 5

1. A Strict Jewish Family: A Girl Eager
   for Precision 7

2. The Philosophy of Being: Edith's Path
   to the Faith 15

3. The Meaning of Existence: Encounter with Teresa
   of Avila and Baptism 27

4. Edith's Rejection of Subjectivism 37

5. The Way of Complete Surrender 47

6. Edith's Prayer During the Gathering Storm 57

7. The Haven of Carmel 67

8. The Science of the Cross: Offering,
   Persecution, Exile and Death 79

9. The Message of Edith Stein 97

Notes 101

Preface

I have chosen to write the biography of this martyred German Jewish woman for three reasons, all of which pierce right to the heart of the drama of our times in its totality and show this drama to be human and spiritual. These three reasons combine to form the center of Edith Stein's personal drama.

Edith was every inch a philosopher, an intellectual. She was called upon to sacrifice herself and she consented wholeheartedly. But she was asked to give up much more than her life, for such a sacrifice would be and was of brief duration. Edith agreed to sacrifice her intellectual activity—her special gift—because God asked this of her through the Rule of her convent, which was the voice of the Church and therefore the will of God.

Edith Stein was an existentialist philosopher. She took part in the first beginnings of this movement. Working in the very heart of existentialism, she came to examine its depth and gauge its truth values.

This existentialist philosopher sought no mitigated form of the Church's spiritual life; she sought no kind of slanted Catholic thought, nor any thought that made compromises with so-called "modern ideas." In religion she lived the perfect spiritual life of prayer and contemplation. She studied St. Thomas Aquinas, the traditional philosopher of the Church, and felt that he expressed her own conclusions on God and the world better than anyone else. She was certain that the Church best answered the "modern" questions.

Through her seemingly plotted-out vocation, Edith Stein answered the most puzzling questions of our times. During her religious life, Edith declared that the most stringent philosophy of the Church had solved her particular philosophical difficulties. As an existentialist, she took up the philosophy of being and found the key to existence in it. She discovered and offered us the united and inseparable aspects of the all-powerful and all-loving One: prayer, truth and total being. Armed with the faith and the most rigorous thought, she grappled with the material world in all its dimensions and answered its problems. From the beginning to the end, this daughter of the Jewish faith made absolutely no compromises with God, herself or the age in which she lived.

She mapped out the long journey from absolute exigency to the boundless response, as did some other women, such as Raissa Maritain and Simone Weil—to mention two whom I once knew. How can Catholics today not be inspired by such examples as theirs?

Edith Stein taught us one final lesson: her first glimpse into the Catholic faith at the Adolph Reinach home was of two people converted during the First World War. Thus, she teaches us that the Catholic Church continues to live in the heart of the "modern world," in which we believe that everything is renewed at each instant.

Edith, we are always in your debt; you brought to the Church the message of your Jewish forbears, the philosophical message of the most "modern" of philosophical movements. We are mindful of this fact from the very outset.

Chapter 1
A Strict Jewish Family
A Girl Eager for Precision

October 12, 1891, on the Jewish Feast of the Expiation, called the Atonement,[1] a girl was born in Breslau, Silesia, into a Jewish family of strict observance and deep faith. Her father, Siegfried Stein, had been in the timber business there for about a year; her mother's name was Augusta Courant. Both parents had come from large families. The Steins had had twenty-two children (from three mothers); the Courants, fourteen.

Edith was barely two years old when Siegfried Stein died, leaving his wife with seven children to care for by running his timber concern. Edith was the youngest of these children.

People said that if this business had not already been prosperous when she inherited it from her husband, Frau Stein would soon have made it so. She knew how to judge standing timber and could buy up whole forests. She made business trips across Silesia and into the Balkans.

While running her business, Augusta Stein would still take time off to bake the family's bread. She was still managing her household at the age of eighty-eight.

It was difficult going for Augusta at first, but not for long. Soon Frau Stein bought a fine stone house, and the

children were able to continue their education uninter-
rupted. The eldest, Elsa, taught for a time and then married. One of the boys, Paul, became a baker, while a
second, Arno, helped his mother run the timber business.
A second daughter, Erika, married and after a time left
her husband to return home to live with her mother. Rosa
stayed at home, and another daughter, Erna, became a
doctor.

In Germany, particularly in Silesia, the years from 1890
to 1900 were years for the massive development of indus-
try and commerce. The era of Bismarck bore fruit. The
Jewish world of Germany might easily have become swal-
lowed up and forgotten in the great commercial expan-
sion, and in fact many Jews did actually lose their faith or
downplay the religious side of their lives. But the Steins
did not and remained staunchly loyal to their faith. The
atmosphere of their household was one of both work and
strict religious observance: prayer and worship. They
prayed in Hebrew before and after meals and often prayed
the incomparable Prayer of Solomon, which expressed
the hope "that all the people of the earth might come to
know that the Eternal is God and that there is no other."

They fasted when it was proper for them to do so and
followed the other obligations of their religion. They
washed their dishes as prescribed. But above all, God
was present to them. "My mother believed in God with
all her heart," wrote Edith's sister, Erna Biberstein, "and
she had complete confidence in him." Much later, when
Edith, then a Catholic, went with her mother to the synagogue to ease the pain of her conversion and the rabbi
read the traditional text: "Hear, O Israel, your God is
One," Frau Stein repeated it back to Edith, alluding to the
dogma of the Holy Trinity.

Edith would later write that she was able to read right
conduct—how to live—in her mother's heart. There she

saw faith and love of God with all the interior strength and intensity that make up the Jewish temperament. From her early years, Edith knew that if there were a God, he had to be loved and served with the same determination and honesty.

The Day of Atonement, Edith's birthday, was the last of the ten days called in the Jewish calendar the "Bitter Days" or the "Austere Days." It is the height of the Jewish spiritual year. On that day, a Jewish person kneels down and "there does what he refused to do before the king of the Persians. He does what no power on earth could move him to do, what he does at no other time of the year before anyone, not even God. And if he kneels, it is not to confess a fault or beg forgiveness of sins, though this is the purpose of the feast. Rather, he kneels because he recognizes the immediate nearness of God.... The Day of Atonement, the crowning point of the ten days of redemption, is justly called the Sabbath of Sabbaths. The assembly quickens to the awareness of the divine presence when it calls to mind the Temple of former days, particularly that moment when the High Priest, on this singular occasion of the year, pronounced the unfathomable name of God, unspoken at any other time except indirectly."[2]

Born on the Day of Atonement, the child Edith was destined to ascend to "the immediate nearness of God" and to call him by name, not just once, but daily. There is a direct bond and an unswerving union between the One God—but One in Three—and Edith Stein of Breslau, who was destined to become one of the foremost philosophers of the twentieth century and the bride of the Lord.

Those who knew Edith before her conversion have depicted her as "cold and distant." One schoolgirl friend described her as "always unnoticed among us, in spite of her reputation for extreme intelligence.... She seemed somewhat old-fashioned to us...always sitting up front in the auditorium, a mere slip of a girl—tiny, almost insignificant, and absorbed in the intensity of her thoughts. Her hair was dull and sleek and she wore it coifed in headbands and fastened together at the neck in a heavy bun. She had an almost sickly pallor, and her large black eyes, with their intense gaze, became stern—almost distant—as if fighting off all distractions.

"But as soon as one got to know her personally, an indescribable kindliness lit up her eyes and a delightful smile animated her face. These little traits hinted at the candor and timidity of childhood. One cannot say she was beautiful or even pretty, nor that she possessed that womanly charm which is so attractive.... But there was something incomparable in her face, from the high intellectual forehead to the marvelously expressive childlike traits—a refreshing glow—difficult not to admire."[3]

I never knew Edith Stein. But as I read these lines I cannot help but think back to two other women, Raissa Maritain and Simone Weil, whom I knew and whose spiritual development so paralleled Edith's. There is that same lessening of strong physical appearance in deference to intellectual and spiritual might—even the profound intensity of gaze which expresses the soul with, perhaps, some of Simone Weil's impetuous will for expression that Edith did not at first have. Simone Weil kept her eyes open first on the world and then later on souls, while Edith lifted hers right up to God. Edith's was a contemplative vocation and this interior call seems evident from childhood. She found strength in silence and an interior life which would culminate in communication with God. The days Edith were to spend in prayer and contemplation before the Blessed Sacrament are signs of this. The interior life governed everything about her and showed up beautifully in her relations with people

whom she treated with the fullness of charity. Simone
Weil progressed from humanity to God; Edith encountered humanity through God.

Edith possessed the spirit of empathy. Sister Aldegonde
Jaegerschmidt noted Edith's knack for teaching as she
helped students who were lost in the vocabulary of
Husserl, giving them introductory notions by which they
could find themselves. "She formed us with endless patience, an attentive and quiet generosity. Always friendly,
without the least irony of criticism, she welcomed our
awkward questions with such a calm, even temper and
dedication that we would scarcely give her a minute's
peace.... Untiringly, she nudged us a little further along
the forbidding path to intellectual knowledge. The zeal
that consumed her won our hearts."[4]

One person who knew Edith before her conversion
shows her at that time viewing creatures with a "detached, penetrating expression, the very bearing of a
judge." She "gave us the impression of a wholly inte-
grated personality in full control of itself."

Thoughts of despair and confusion had no part in
Edith Stein's conversion. Neither did the discontent pe-
culiar to those who search "elsewhere" for the balance
they cannot find here. Hers was an intellectual conviction
and a judgment of the world, its existence and its meaning. One might say that Edith's conversion was not *psychological*, a conversion based on personal needs, but that
it was both *intellectual* and *spiritual*, the two being united
and constantly parallel. The judgment of her mind and
the desire of her soul looked for God as the one necessity
for existence—not so much her own existence among
humankind, but the existence of all creation, the existence of the whole world acknowledging its source and
meaning. The physical portrait of Edith has already told
us what her whole life would constantly stress.

As a child, Edith had a yearning for the absolute that was later to govern her thought. This desire for the absolute first showed up in a childhood disappointment. Brought up with brothers and sisters of all ages, she not only joined in their games, but wished to understand them. The games enhanced her mental precocity, and when she was sent to nursery-school at the age of four because she wanted to go to school "like the other children," she returned home defeated and disconsolate because of the infantile atmosphere of the school.

Carrying her in his arms, her elder brother would teach her the names of the German poets and the titles of their works. When the family played the game called *Dichter-quartett*,[5] the child of four amazed guests because she knew the names of the authors and could match them with their works. At this age, her companions thought her "deep, reserved, quiet" but "always obliging and understanding." And once, when she did not get the very highest marks at school, she said at home, "Mother, forgive me for not getting the best grades. Hilda did, and that's better, because she doesn't have any mother." The absolute of understanding could conceive of giving way only to the absolute of charity.

Edith began school on her sixth birthday, October 12, in the middle of the school year, which began at Easter.[6] In spite of this disadvantage, by Christmas she was one of the very best in the class.

In 1906, when she was fifteen, Edith left school. We might ask why. She had received the highest marks, but had never been given the first place, which all her companions insisted she deserved. Her biographers think the headmaster's anti-Semitism can account for that. At any rate, she went to live with her married sister, Elsa, by now the mother of three, to help with the housekeeping. But she was quick to learn that this kind of life was not for her. Edith returned home to her mother and made up for lost time by special tutoring. She passed the *Studienanstalt* in 1908, and in 1911 the final comprehensive examinations that led to higher studies.[7]

Frau Stein's remarkable personality dominated Edith's life at home. Edith later wrote, "At home it was not exactly a matter of education. As children we read right conduct in our mother's example as if in a mirror of virtues. Mother taught us the horror of sin. And when she said 'That's a sin,' she conveyed the idea of everything hateful and ugly and we lived in dread of it."[8]

Edith's studies gave her a well-rounded education. She was fluent in French, English, Spanish, Latin, Greek and, of course, Hebrew. At twenty, she enrolled at the University of Breslau to take courses in history, philosophy and experimental psychology.

Quite early in life Edith lost her Jewish religion, denying the very existence of God. However, she continued to accompany her mother to the synagogue to spare her the pain of a daughter's disbelief.

In Breslau she read Husserl's *Logical Investigations*, which quickened her mind to a train of thought that would become her own. Because Husserl taught at Göttingen, she went there to continue her higher education. Her mother's cousin, Richard Courant, himself a professor of mathematics at the university, welcomed her.

"I was twenty-one," wrote Edith, "and full of eager anticipation. Psychology had deceived me. I had come to the conclusion that this science was still in its infancy and lacked an objective foundation. But the little I knew of phenomenology delighted me, particularly the objective method of investigation."

In her opinion, phenomenology was Husserl. And he taught at Göttingen. Her family had raised no objections to her studying there, so she embarked upon the intellectual journey that was to influence her until her recognition of the first and complete reality, which is God.

As was the tradition, her classmates made up a song about Edith when she left Breslau. They titled it: "The Objective Expert." Objectivity was just coming to the fore in the philosophical world. Kantian and post-Kantian idealism had long dominated the entire German intellectual scene. At the same time, experimental psychology, a discipline that attracted Edith's attention, was totally limited to observation of exterior human acts. The human person seemed torn between the distant world of abstract ideas and a reality limited only to what the senses could directly perceive. How could someone like Edith, driven by that impassioned search for truth, put up with a dichotomy of being that could never lead to any religious faith?

Chapter 2

The Philosophy of Being
Edith's Path to the Faith

Love and intellectual conviction were at the root of Edith Stein's conversion. If this seems paradoxical, let us see how and why her conversion is one of the most significant in the drama of modern Catholicism.

Her conversion came about through love and not emotionalism. Edith Stein suffered a great deal: this is certain. She endured much all her life, and even early in life—as when the headmaster refused to acknowledge her superiority in school, apparently because of anti-Semitism. Yet when she returned home, instead of brooding and crying over this injustice, she would try to find reasons to justify it to her mother so that she could rejoice in her schoolmate's success. She suffered intensely when she attended the synagogue with her mother after she had lost her faith. Edith suffered when she sensed her mother's grief over her daughter's "infidelity." She endured great pain in the heartache she caused her mother with her conversion to Catholicism, departure from home, and entrance into the religious life. She suffered still more during the Nazi persecutions.

Edith never expressed the grief welling up from within her soul. Her love was totally foreign to any emotionalism in the bad sense, because hers was a contemplative love. How else can one explain Edith's ecstasy before her God in the Eucharist, her complete absorption in his infinite presence? We do not find it difficult to depict this girl who rarely showed her feelings, wholly *absorbed* in the contemplation of Him-Who-Is. Nothing but love could sustain such a silent dialogue.

The sharpened edge of her intellect came to recognize its cause and final end—this was the food of her dialogue with God. Her intellect saw the infinite necessity of an infinite being who is infinite love. She contemplated him and listened to him speak to her mind the language of absolute presence and absolute necessity, in which she saw her origin.

This small woman's response to the infinite showed her the Being without whom she would be nothing.

At Göttingen, the philosopher Edmund Husserl, one of the first teachers of phenomenology and existentialism, opened her mind to the revelation of being.

Almost by sheer chance Edith had begun to read Husserl's *Logical Investigations*, and this same chance brought her and Erna to their cousin's home in Göttingen.

This "bit of chance" was to open whole new horizons to Edith and quell one of her deepest longings: "Psychology had deceived me. I had come to the conclusion that this science was still in its infancy and lacked an objective foundation. But the little I knew of phenomenology delighted me, particularly the objective method of investigation." In a world of idealism and relativism that questioned the validity of the mind, she suddenly caught the glimmering of a light, and something dared whisper the words "reality" and "truth" to her. Edith accepted and turned wholeheartedly toward this light.

When Husserl delivered several lectures at the Sorbonne in 1929, one of his listeners, Benjamin Fondane, described him this way: "He is neither a miracle-worker nor a preacher. Beneath the guise of a humble person from the outlying districts is a man who radiates the virtues of order and decency. You could call his attitude shyness if there hadn't been something attractive and provocative about his bespectacled appearance. He pretends to be but a man of science, mindful only of *describing* the laws and basic structures of consciousness, hesitant to delve into reality or get into its way, trying to be rigorous by readily accepting everything, exaggerating nothing if possible, but overlooking nothing.... His modesty comes from the fact that he serves us absolute truth and not his own truth."[1]

"This humble provincial" was to set Edith in the right direction. Because he wanted only to "describe reality," he "ignored nothing and believed not in *his* truth, but in an *absolute truth....*"

At Göttingen Husserl taught Edith that "truth is an absolute," that it "is not the creation of one who perceives it."[2] He taught that one must discover in oneself the primary truths upon which the entire structure of universal knowledge rests.[3] When he asked how he could seriously question himself about how to escape from the island of his consciousness, since it was clearly evident that his consciousness could attain to objective meaning, he ran up against what had obstructed every philosophy of reality and existence from the time of Descartes and gave rise to countless idealisms and relativisms that were but various disguises for skepticism.[4] He resolved that he could get away from the island of his consciousness, but said it would be folly to try to define a state of consciousness because the very structure of life remains when the "phenomena" pass away and the "structure" evades all one's doubt and relativism. There is a "universal foundation for the experience of the ego."

Edith was attracted to Husserl's desire to investigate things as they are[5] to find out what they have to tell us, as Husserl himself stated and the second great phenomenologist, Heidegger, reiterated.

At Juvisy in 1932, almost twenty years after Edith went to Göttingen, a German Benedictine monk, Dom Feuling, working with the *Société de Philosophie Thomiste*, explained the phenomenological thinkers to the German Catholic world. In the course of his work he outlined Husserl's basic ideas with these words: "This work will be complete only when it leads us to the first origin of all that is created, to the first being in that and through that all other beings...with their actions and their objects, are originally constituted—to the truly absolute ego who alone constitutes everything and who is himself uncreated—to God, who lives his life in creating...."

Edith Stein immediately perceived Husserl's desire to advance beyond all philosophical systems and reach out to the heart of true reality and the foundation of life. She was, of course, unaware that her path led to God, "creating everything that is created," as Dom Feuling illustrated. Without realizing it, she desired to discover the *Source* of all reality.

When Edith helped out at Juvisy in 1932, she spoke of Husserl's work in this vein: "The phenomenological method is a process of *revelation* that transcends the world as we know it—it is a description of actions and of bodies of actions...." And, mentioning without emphasis that she had not followed Husserl's philosophical evolution, Edith Stein noted during her "Days at Juvisy" that what had characterized Husserl's early pupils in the Göttingen period, herself included, was an orientation into the meaning of objective essences that had in due course given the impression of a Scholastic renewal.[6]

Husserl's philosophy is a praise of the concrete, as for

example when he spoke of a red object's "redness" as the red object itself and not the abstraction of the genus "redness." He said we perceive an object as it is. No amount of rationalization can make one hold objects as non-existent because it is the mind itself that perceives them. Husserl wrote that the only truly absolute being was the pure intellect.[7]

At Juvisy, Edith Stein spoke of the "plenitude of essence and being that in every true experience pervades the subject of the experience and, extending beyond the evidence of the consciousness, escapes every possibility of grasping it." It was extremely important for her to realize this. It shows that she had immediately seen in Husserl's work the mind's immediate awareness of the existence of the world, that is, a grasp so direct upon the reality of the world, that no sophism can undo it. At the same time, we begin to see the direction of her thought: we are aware of the existence of the universe; it *pervades* us and eludes our every attempt to "grasp and express it"; God speaks to us in the reality of the world's existence; he is there, behind all things, he and he alone Who Is. Therefore, to be receptive to the voice of the world speaking to one's consciousness is to be receptive to God, to hear him speaking. Edith had soared to the very brink of contemplation.

Because Husserl had not resolved his intuition[8] to its ultimate conclusion and avoided such a conclusion by putting the question of the actual existence of the interior world as perceived by the mind "into parentheses," he shut himself off from the only effective way out of idealism and skepticism. This, Jacques Maritain has conclusively shown us.[9] Edith perfected Husserl's philosophy by seeing there is no third way between the acceptance and refusal of the reality of existence and that if, through our "consciousness," we come into contact with something, we must surely admit that something does in fact exist.

In 1913, Edith went to Göttingen to attend Husserl's lectures. She found a small university town, encircled by forested hillsides. Romantic castles dominated the Weser Valley and thick walls hemmed the city. The town-hall was Gothic in design, and the central square displayed the traditional water fountain. One of the Hanseatic cities, Göttingen was steeped in an ever-present sense of history. The Grimm brothers had studied there, as well as Heine and Bismarck.

At Göttingen the students made the most of the life in the streets and taverns, while they hid their rooms behind windows of stained bottle glass. On regularly scheduled evenings they sang in the taverns and held their customary meetings, to which the young men came decked out in traditional hats and ribbons and wearing swords at their sides.

Edith Stein came to Göttingen on April 17, when in her twenty-first year, with her friend Rosa Guttmann, a mathematician. They took two rooms at a boarding house, setting aside one of these as a living and work-room.

Edith rarely mixed in at such student festivities as dance nights, ritually scheduled for Wednesdays and Sundays. Instead, she would tramp up and down through the nearby forests and wander over the foothills of the Hartz Mountains—"seas of stone" and "haunted rocks" where sorcerers once gathered to dance on the nights of the Witches' Sabbath. It was not only in textbooks that Edith sought the meaning of the world; she searched also in nature, with which she was keenly in harmony.

Because Husserl was a professor, it was not his place to meet a young, unknown student. He left such matters to his assistant, Adolf Reinach, who was thirty years old at that time—and fated to die shortly afterwards in World

War I. Reinach was Jewish, as were many of Germany's philosophers in that era.

The Reinachs were an upper-class Jewish family, but despite all his advantages, Adolf lived in a kind of strange sadness that nothing seemed to justify. He was married and deeply in love, considerate to all who knew him, beloved by all. His sadness may have been due to this: he had not yet discovered the genuine hope that he searched for so intensely. He bravely examined the world to discover this hope. "One must not be afraid of ultimate realities," he said. But it seemed to him that the night was filled with the gelatinous and gloomy mass of pantheism. This very interesting man had set out on the road ahead of Edith, and providence had led her to him.

For quite some time Adolf Reinach lived at the brink of Christian faith. He wrote that Christianity was "the meeting place of all the great classical developments" and admitted to Dietrich von Hildebrand that the Trinity is the only acceptable concept of God.[10] However, Reinach did not truly embrace the faith until 1915, after several months at the warfront. He wrote to his wife, also on the verge of conversion, "The first weeks were frightening. Then God's peace came into me and now all is well."

The Reinach whom Edith Stein met was still a restless, intense man. She wrote, "Never have I been received with such kindness by anyone.... It was as though a whole new world had opened up to me."

Several days later, Edith met Husserl in person and he struck her the same way, according to Alexandre Koyré— a pupil of his at the time[11]—as one who surprised everyone who listened to him. He had the knack of uprooting them from the mire of skepticism by showing them a glimpse of reality.

From Koyré to Dietrich von Hildebrand, everyone agreed that Husserl soon took note of Edith and began paying her special attention. Frau Husserl was more difficult to win over, but Edith succeeded, though that woman "had the habit of perplexing her husband's best pupils with her incisive and ironic remarks."

Edith continued her classes at Göttingen with Max Scheler and apparently received her first glimmer of the light of the Gospels through him. Everything seemed to direct her toward the study of human life in its reality; Scheler's philosophy was indeed a cry of one alone in the wilderness. He studied the degrees of sympathy, the meanings of suffering, relationships between beings, the meaning of resentment and heroism, wisdom and holiness. At a time when philosophy was but the history of reason and ideas, reflections on scientific knowledge or on the birth-pangs of society, Scheler was a true precursor.

Scheler's life, devoted to the study of the tragic in human existence, would itself develop into a tragedy, like that of Kierkegaard, his forerunner. Through his mother's side of the family, he was Jewish. At some point, he received baptism, but shortly afterwards he got caught up in the whirlwind of a passionate love affair, married a divorcee and cut himself off from the Church. The reverberations of his conjugal life forced him to relinquish his professorship at the university. He began to teach in a small Göttingen cafe, and to visit Beuron Abbey to try to find the peace of mind that finally came with his re-entry into the Church.[12] Edith, who wrote of herself, "the thirst for truth was my only prayer," listened to Scheler more closely than to Husserl. "He was an extremely fascinating man," she wrote. "He even looked like a genius. I have never experienced the phenomenon of genius in any other person. He was handsome and his blue eyes seemed to radiate the glow of a higher world. Yet, his life left its etchings on his noble features and made one think—irresistibly—of Oscar Wilde's *A Por-*

trait of Dorian Gray.... He spoke with great emphasis, sometimes dramatically, and always captivated his audience."

This zealous girl went after truth with all her might. She decided to write her thesis on the *Einfühling*—a difficult word to translate. Sometimes "empathy" suffices, but we rather think it could be called "intuition by sympathy."

Edith explained her choice: "In his course on nature and spirit, Husserl maintained that one could only experience an objective external world intersubjectively—that is, by a plurality of knowing individuals who can communicate experiences with one another. Such an exterior world presupposes the experience of other individuals. Husserl, following Theodore Lipps, called this experience *Einfühling* (empathy), but did not explain what it consisted of. This was a gap worth filling: I wanted to find out what empathy meant."

Edith devoted her work to the study of human relationships and their meaning. Scheler had crossed her path at just the right moment. He gave her much more than a philosophical contribution, for he planted in her mind an idea that constantly grew: "For myself, as for many others," she wrote, "his influence extended far beyond the bounds of philosophy. I do not know in what year Scheler returned to the Catholic Church, but it cannot have been long afterwards, for he was overflowing with Christian ideas and conveyed them with all the brilliance of his mind and with great power of expression. For me it was the unfolding of a whole new world, which until then had remained completely unknown to me. But this still did not lead me to the faith. Aside from that, he did open up a vast new realm of phenomena before my eyes and I could no longer ignore it.... The fetters of the rationalism in which I had been brought up without realizing it shook loose and I suddenly found myself encountering the world of faith. People with whom I came into contact every day and whom I admired lived in that world, and I thought that it at least deserved some investigation. I made no systematic examination into this religion, because my mind was still too absorbed with other things. I remained open to the influences of my environment and accepted their influence almost without noticing it."

She was receptive to her environment because it satisfied needs of which she was hardly aware. A bond was being knotted, a sheaf of wheat gathered together for the harvest. From Husserl she learned that the mind reveals the existence of a profound reality that sustains existence. Scheler taught her that we cannot really experience the reality of the world except in relation to others, who illuminate us with a sense of presence because it is a relationship of love, an expression of harmony toward... toward what? That profound reality sustaining the universe. What do you call it? What is this Being that is more intensely in existence than all creation, the Being that gives creation its own being and reveals its own existence?

During these months, as always, Edith took note of life going on around her, and Scheler taught her what being aware of others meant. While on a hike up in the mountains, she unexpectedly had to stay at a farm overnight. In the morning she awoke to the sound of the household at prayer before beginning the day's work. That unknown reality was there among them, present to them and shared in by them.

During her years at Göttingen, Edith frequently took time off from her studies to trek through the countryside of Protestant Thuringia and the Hartz, taking note of Luther's influence. She visited Weimar and the tombs of

Goethe and Schiller, the results of a rationalistic or romantic philosophy thought to be the apex of human wisdom. But she was following another path on her way to truth.

In 1914, the war interrupted her intellectual life, but she patched together what she could when Husserl, newly appointed to Freiburg, asked her to accompany him as his assistant. She accepted. The One who was patiently calling and waiting for her had a special destiny mapped out for her.

That same summer of 1916, while Edith lived at Freiburg, Adolf and Anna Reinach decided to become Christians—Protestants. Reinach questioned his motives: "Might it be that I am not yet ready to join the Catholic Church?" Anna, who would later become a Catholic, thought that "once we were in communion with Christ, he would lead us where he willed."

The following November, Adolf was killed in Flanders. Soon afterwards, Anna asked Edith to arrange his philosophical papers. It frightened Edith to think of going to the Reinach home and finding there, instead of "a happy young couple," only the somber shadows of deep mourning. To her surprise, "far from being disconsolate," Anna herself lent strength to her late husband's friends—"on account of her unshakable faith in the living God."

"It was my first encounter with the cross," Edith confided much later, "and with the divine strength it inspires in those who carry it. For the first time, I saw the Church born out of the passion of Christ and victorious over death. At that moment my unbelief was utterly crushed. Judaism paled before my eyes and the light of Christ poured into my heart—the light of Christ in the mystery of the cross. Because of this light, I desired to take the habit of the Carmel that I might be called into the 'Order of the Cross.'"

Seven years were to pass before her baptism on January 1, 1922. But the two converging paths of philosophical and human evidence, of philosophical and human necessity, had finally met. The existence of the world was a fact that intellectual awareness can recognize and encounter, but the underlying reality, the essential Being, is he who gave Anna and Adolf Reinach the grace to be what they were because they were of and in the Church.

Observing the bond between Anna and her deceased husband, Edith noted: "At that moment, my unbelief left me." It was not because of a vague recognition of an unknown spiritual power, but because of the strength of Christ and his cross, in which the Church shares. Therein lay the source of Anna Reinach's peace and of the prayer that the peasants joyfully shared before setting off to work.

Chapter 3

The Meaning of Existence
Encounter with Teresa of Avila and Baptism

On August 3, 1916, Edith Stein passed the oral examination of her thesis at the University of Freiburg, where Husserl taught under a full professorship, and she received her degree under him *summa cum laude*. Edith joyfully took up his offer to be his private assistant. She took Reinach's place, vacant since he had gone off to war and to that he would never return. Among her many new duties, she had to transcribe all of Husserl's shorthand notes.[1] Edith began this undertaking after her encounter with the converted Anna Reinach and after she had arranged Reinach's notes.

There was no apparent change in her. She took her usual long excursions. Now, they were into Freiburg, to the Black Forest and to Lake Constance. Her companions were her sister Erna and Rosa Guttmann. She read a great deal of Stefan George, Goethe and Gottfried Keller.

But Edith had begun turning her mind to more important things. Among Reinach's notes she read: "Everything bears the imprint of God, including time and space." Also, "God, in his mercy, has granted me a new life....

Through prayer, I come into contact with the ultimate cause of the world."² There are two ways to this realization—the mind and the soul—but the light that shines upon one is the same that illumines the other. Guided by Husserl and Reinach, her mind arrived at their same conclusions and her soul, enkindled by the example of the Reinachs, received the revelation like a seed about to quicken into life.

Those who knew Edith well are inclined to describe her as somewhat cold and distant. So it may seem at first glance, but if so, it is only because her love for humanity was deeper than mere emotional display. She wanted to lavish on the world that "sympathy" on which Max Scheler had focused his attention and research. She expected the same treatment in return, but in a much more profound expression than mere effusive cordiality. She desired to base her encounter with the world in her love for creation.

"The love I encounter in my life," she wrote, "strengthens and develops me, giving me the power to do unheard of things. If the mistrust I sometimes have to contend with paralyzes all my creative ability, affection and understanding kindness, on the other hand, love brings me such a rich treasure that I can share it with others without fear of exhausting myself in doing so."

When she noted Husserl's students struggling with his lofty and exceedingly difficult teachings, Edith found the way to express her desire to help others by organizing introductory courses in phenomenology. But when someone asked if it were true that she taught philosophy at Freiburg, she replied, "No. I'm satisfied with running a kindergarten for would-be philosophers." The future Sister Aldegonde Jaegerschmidt saw this helpfulness in Edith when she described Edith's "knack for teaching" and training pupils "with endless patience, an attentive and quiet generosity. Always friendly, without the least irony or criticism, she welcomed our awkward questions with such a calm, even temper and dedication, that we would scarcely give her a minute's peace.... Untiringly, she nudged us a little further along the forbidding path to intellectual knowledge. The zeal that consumed her won our hearts. We were heady with the sheer joy of learning."

Husserl fell sick in the autumn of 1918, and at his request Edith read to him from the Bible. He had reached the very threshold of the faith and spoke as a man of deep religious convictions: "The life of man is only a progression toward God," he said to one of his students. "I tried to reach this progression toward God without theological proofs or methods—in other words, I tried to reach God without God's help." Edith must have seen the impossibility of such a task.

Husserl added, "I tried in one way or another to delete God from my scientific thought so that I might outline a way to him for those who lack the security of faith in the Church that we have." He clearly saw that such as a method of procedure would have been disastrous for him, had he not had "a deep attachment to God and belief in Christ to hold on to."

Edith was quite far removed from Husserl. During this period, Husserl's philosophy took a turn toward pure interior experience and a philosophy of consciousness. It was no longer in touch with the reality of existence that had so attracted Edith.

New horizons were opening for Edith. She returned to Breslau and, in February of 1919, Husserl presented her with a kind of "certificate"—a glowing testimony about the quality of her philosophical teachings and a token of his appreciation for all the work she had done for him. Edith requested a lecturing position at Göttingen and completed her psychological projects, which were published in the *1922 Yearbook*. In them she applied her analysis to real-life situations, such as weariness and feverishness, and observed that these phenomena could be governed by the mental attitude we take in life.

She expressed her deep concern about the meaning of her existence, the secret of which she had not yet uncovered. This interior duality nourished her psychological experience with riches that examination of other phenomena would not have revealed. Thus, she wrote, "I can ardently desire religious faith without receiving it." Also, "Suppose a totally convinced atheist experiments with the existence of God because of a religious experience. He could be totally oblivious of faith while investigating it. He forbids it to act within him, but clings instead to his scientific vision of the world that would shrink before an unchecked faith."[3]

Like Scheler, Husserl, Gabriel Marcel in France and Karl Jaspers as well (though in a different way),[4] Edith Stein encountered faith as a *living experience*, an experience founded on truth. At this point she broke away from the rationalism of the preceding age. It was not a question of a struggle with concepts or with ideas void of human "meaning." The time when man was reduced to what he "thought" had come to an end. It was finished and done with, because such an outlook could give life no real meaning. Suddenly, the life of faith reappeared as truth in the very center of creation in the lives of persons who wanted, certainly, *to think*, but rightly *to think in terms of the whole of life*.

The same "experience"—if one may call it that—would find a parallel in the second generation of psychoanalysts—Jung, for example. They observed faith in their analyses of the living human being and looked upon it as a balancing factor and the realization of truth in existence. Thus, a psychoanalyst like Jung would come to recognize that the themes of faith (especially Catholicism) best correspond to the interior appeal of human life.[5]

As we have seen exemplified in her childhood, the mind and soul of Edith Stein were razor-sharp. Husserl read the Bible and saw the "obstacle" but hedged about it. Reinach jumped the hurdle. Edith Stein's keen logic would do the same. Hers was a twofold logic: that of the intellect and that of the soul. If faith, the *explanation* of being, held the key to the mystery of the universe, her soul had to cleave to it, but it could not unless her intellect had arrived at the same conclusion. Man's existence is a unity and Edith threw herself into the quest for the whole human person.

We easily see that Edith *was already living the life of faith*, and never will the statement: "You would not look for me if you had not already found me" find so true a personification as in her. But Edith required both mind and soul to find a common resting place, so that her soul might partake of everything reached through her mind, and her mind could verify everything her soul perceived. Which moved which: mind or soul? They both supported and constantly converged upon one another. Perhaps her mind first recognized the demands of truth, the necessity of going back to the source of being, but—and this is important to see—her soul had already advanced far into the perception and meditation of the mystery of being.

After her request for a lecturing position at Göttingen had been turned down, Edith spent the summer of 1921 with a friend, Frau Conrad-Martius, and her husband at their farm in the Palatinate. Like Edith, Hedwig Conrad-Martius had been one of Husserl's most promising pupils. Their work together had united them in a deep friendship. Though Hedwig Martius was Protestant, her library contained more than one Catholic book, among which was *The Life of St. Teresa of Avila, Written by Herself.* One evening in that summer of 1921, Edith was alone at the farm and picked up the autobiography. She read all night long and finished it in the early morning, exclaiming, "There is truth!"

We do not consider this to be a premature enlightenment. Her mind had been prepared for it in advance through Scheler and Reinach. It was rather a convergence all at once perceived—a kind of illumination, naturally— between what Edith had felt developing in her and the spiritual experience of the Saint of Carmel.

Frau Conrad-Martius described the kind of life they led together at the farm: "We wanted to live in the deeply-rooted spiritual ideal of poverty as much as possible. I remember that one day we were carrying coal, when Professor Koyré came to pay us a visit. He was beside himself at the sight of women doing such heavy work.

"After nightfall we were far too exhausted to discuss philosophy and, apart from the few times our friends came to see us, we usually spent our evenings darning or sewing...or retiring early." Frau Conrad-Martius adds, "Edith's development had been slowed, because even though she had a Christian outlook on life, she had not directly come to grips with the problem of faith." She goes on to say that Edith "was a good and wise woman with unflagging devotion.... She remained secretive and quiet.... She always looked abstracted, as though absorbed in an unbroken meditation.... We were the closest of friends, but I know nothing of any consequence that I can say about her interior evolution."[6]

Her "unbroken meditation"—a meditation profound and existential—so enveloped the whole of her existence that it could not be shared with others. Her reading of St. Teresa was but the consequence of her "meditation."

We have a text written during this meditative period which appeared after her conversion in 1927: "I am making plans for the future," Edith wrote, "and am arranging my immediate life accordingly. But I am deeply convinced that there is something looming in the offing that will upset all my projects. I mean the true and living faith which I still refuse to assent to, which I prevent from becoming active within me."

She, the creature, had been summoned: she had heard the divine voice and knew that it was directed to her personally. Belief quickened within her and she felt the existence of the infinite Creator. How, then, could she still balk at taking the final step? Such a refusal of truth was so unlike her. We shall understand Edith's position better if we picture her waiting until she had become absolutely certain that her whole being could accept the faith, so she would be able to take that final plunge totally, in complete certitude and perfect understanding of the final "Yes," that *Fiat* to the whole body of revealed truth.

The continuation of Edith's text leaves absolutely no doubt that in this period she had lived a truly spiritual experience: "There exists a state of repose in God, a total suspension of all mental activity in which one can make neither plans nor decisions, in which one can do nothing, but in which, having given over all things to the divine will, one surrenders entirely to one's destiny. *I have experienced this state somewhat, following an experience that, exceeding all my own abilities, totally consumed my spiritual energies and divested me of all possible action. Compared to the cessation of activity rising from lack of strength, repose in God is something at once new and indomitable. Previously, it was the silence of death, but this gave way to a feeling of intimate security and release from all anxiety,* obligation and responsibility in relation to action. And while I gave myself up to this feeling, *a new life began little by little to pour into me* and—without forcing my will—urged me again to action. This vital onrush seems to come from an activity and a force that is not mine and which, without doing violence to what is mine, becomes active within me. The only condition for such a spiritual rebirth seems to be a certain receptivity which is at the very basis of the individual who is aloof from any kind of psychical mechanism."

Ten years later, Bergson would say that the mystical soul falls silent, as though listening to a voice calling it, then immediately surrenders itself. The soul, said Bergson, does not *directly perceive the force* that overpowers it, but only senses its undefinable presence. A great mystic's soul does not come to a halt in ecstasy, but is in *repose*, although while it awaits another impulse, there is a movement, an excitement within it.[8] Is not this what Edith Stein felt happening within her?

Edith still refused to seek baptism and even went so far as to believe that she "refused to consent to the faith." However, by this time she was decidedly committed to the world of grace and faith—infinite grace—the grace that was working within her "as in a glass darkly."

Because she had actually *arrived* at faith, can we not say that during the long silence between her encounter with Reinach's texts and the day she requested baptism, she underwent the "trials"—the dark night of the senses and the soul—that St. John of the Cross described? We know nothing about this, but we are inclined to think she did. The page quoted above does bring to mind the "prayer of quiet" that St. Teresa placed at the beginning of the contemplative life. Another certainty is that in the year preceding her decisive step, Edith Stein sacrificed something very dear to her so she could "keep her heart undivided."

The very morning that she finished reading St. Teresa, Edith set out for a nearby town to buy a small catechism and a missal. God had finally granted what she had been seeking over many months in such a typical way: "My thirst for truth was my only prayer" as well as through the continuous focusing of her soul's attention on the Eucharist.[9]

Henceforth, Edith could say with Teresa: "When the Lord fills us with great favors, the virtues become so alive and love so informed, that one cannot conceal the effects of this divine action...." Real graces shine in us regardless of ourselves, and they are always beneficial to others. That is why the Bridegroom openly tells us: "He has made charity spring up in me."

Edith poured over her little catechism and missal, and one morning, after Mass, she followed the priest into the sacristy and asked him to baptize her.

Edith was received into the Church on January 1, 1922.[10] She spoke her Latin responses loudly and fervently, and Frau Conrad-Martius observed, "The most beautiful thing of all was her childlike happiness." Edith had come home to her Creator: the love dwelling in her soul had responded to the searchings of her mind.

Chapter 4

Edith's Rejection of Subjectivism

It is quite likely that Edith recognized her progression toward baptism long before she requested the sacrament. A longing such as hers would compel one to go all the way to a total commitment in union with him who had given so much. She received Holy Communion on the day of her baptism—and daily from then on. The Bishop of Speyer confirmed her and she selected Canon Schwind as her spiritual director.

Edith suffered an immense heartache in the midst of her great joy, knowing she would have to tell her mother of the conversion. Choosing not to delay over the matter, she went to Breslau, and kneeling before her she said, "Mother, I am a Catholic." The old woman wept and Edith wept with her. To soften the impact of such a blow, Edith lived with her mother for several months, attending the synagogue with her as in the past, but now she read the Psalms in an entirely new light.[1]

Edith had to get back to work once again, and Canon Schwind located a teaching position for her at the Dominican convent school in Speyer. There she taught German grammar and literature, living the life of a religious at the school for eight years (1922-1931). The nuns gave her a small room within the convent itself. It was plainly furnished with a bed, closets, shelves, a dressing table and straight-backed chairs. Here she could follow the convent life, attending Mass the first thing in the morning. Her real life had begun at last. At first she had no other cares except the satisfaction of an insatiable intellectual curiosity. She had attained the God so long sought and daily performed the mission he had entrusted her with. She prayed and received the sacraments. What more could she desire?

Edith was a good and conscientious professor, devoted to her students. She enjoyed seasoning her classes with a great deal of humor. She lived an interior life, eating and sleeping very little and spending long hours at prayer; her prayerful attitude astounded those who saw her then—upright as a statue with a distant and immobile expression on her face. Her students thought she was a little distant and her teaching quite lofty. The inspector who checked up on Edith reprimanded her for not using the new teaching methods that incorporated more student participation. It grieved her to think she had done less than she ought.

Her life at Speyer was troubled, for the noble gift granted her would take second place to nothing. How could she not help but be wholly absorbed in the great blessing of faith given to her in the form of a continual presence? It was *her* faith, *her* presence with God. Still, she recognized the need for more. She talked about entering the Carmel, but her careful director would not hear of it. She was ready for the contemplative life—in fact, she was already a contemplative, but Canon Schwind deemed it wiser for her to go on living as she had. Edith impressed those around her as being physically present with them, but mentally abstracted from them.

She would eventually make a great sacrifice by relinquishing her philosophical studies. Although she did not seem to regret it, we think it incredible to imagine a mind such as Edith's at least not suffering inwardly from not *serving*, because her mind and soul were so bound together and their development had been so parallel. Her mind's desire to serve was not empty intellectual pride— it wanted to serve God, to unite with the Lord in whom it found the meaning of the existence of the universe.

During her spare time, Edith translated the *Letters* and *Journal* of Cardinal Newman with all the care and precision she devoted to everything. Father Przywara, who met Edith through Canon Schwind, immediately sensed the special fiber of her mind and soul. As if translating one of the greatest converts of the modern era were not a thing of mere chance, he touched right on the heart of her problems when he counseled her to study St. Thomas. She had asked him how to begin investigating the Church's philosophy, and he replied, "Begin with St. Thomas right away. Don't bother with manuals or commentaries." This remarkable Jesuit saw that the "Angelic Doctor" would satisfy Edith's mind, already attuned to the profound logic of being and the Source of being. Just as St. Thomas had supported and directed the great mystics of the Carmel—John of the Cross and Teresa—so also he was about to influence Edith by showing her intellect what the Saint of Avila had already taught her soul.

To get her involved in thomism, Father Przywara advised Edith to translate St. Thomas' *Quaestiones Disputatae de Veritate* into German. Since this was quite a difficult undertaking, it brought her much discouragement, and some men of letters—Joseph Pieper for one—upbraided her for occasional obscurities and ambiguities. But Edith tackled something that went far beyond the mechanics of translating when she confronted modern thought with the Church's ancient thought; from this comparison came her own work entitled *Husserl's Phenomenology and the Philosophy of St. Thomas Aquinas.*

She understood that the central thomistic intuition had actually prompted her throughout her intellectual life: the existence of the universe is an incontrovertible reality and we are in its milieu; it exists for us and we for it; the intellect is nothing if not the "captor" of being. Behind the existence of the universe, animating and sustaining it, is an infinite intellect that makes us aware of the universe so that we can interpret and recognize it, discover its meaning and thereby find the reason for our own existence.

Edith was particularly excited by the chapter in *De Veritate* that treats of the way God knows both the universe and himself: all things are totally and absolutely present to him. He has no need of encountering anything in actual experience as we do, or of undergoing the slow and nebulous logical progression from effect to cause. In God, being and knowledge are one and the same: he is all that he knows, he knows all that is, and only what he knows exists.

Edith perceived the universal presence of God in the existence of the world from the very outset of the intellectual search that culminated in her accepting the Catholic faith. This illumination was in keeping with her first philosophical thoughts. The faith she found filled her entirely with certainty, but we should not be taken aback in learning that her religious faith did not set all things up in their proper perspectives. Perhaps she was not really a thomist at first; maybe she assigned too great a value to the will in the development of knowledge; she certainly did confuse theology and philosophy by making philosophy too dependent on theology and nearly subordinating all true knowledge to the faith. Later, she came to sense the "balance" of the "perennial philoso-phy." Regardless of this confusion, she at once grasped the essential point: *ens, verum, bonum convertuntur*—"Be-ing, the true, the good and the convertible." All that exists is true, good and beautiful, and outside of the immense realm of creation there is nothing.

She embraced this truth with all her might. It an-swered one of her earlier questions—about the misery which had befallen her world and was soon to utterly devastate it. As people lose sight of the idea of an objec-tive good, of a natural law imposing rights and duties upon creatures, the shadow of *nothingness*, an empty void, spreads out over the globe. Dostoyevsky and Nietzsche, two opposites, encounter one another at this point. "If there be no God, then all things are allowable," Dostoyevsky made one of his characters exclaim; Nietz-sche resounded with: "God is dead." Then, "all things are allowable," and a great despair will settle over the world: nothing will have meaning and all human acts will only echo the "emptiness" of all else in the world. Borrowing these conclusions from one branch of existen-tialism, the "existential" novelists chanted this mournful dirge.

All her life Edith had known that the mind revealed existence, but if she knew that—and this would explain her early confusion between rational philosophy and the-ology enlightened by faith—if she knew that, this aware-ness had been initially enlightened by her love for the world, to which she had readily opened her heart. In that intense, clear-sighted love for the world, she ascended to the stature of Husserl himself, for in that love she con-demned the entire subjectivistic universe that admittedly depended upon itself in the most hideous of egoisms—intellectual pride. As soon as all things are referred to the "subject," philosophy itself becomes an impossibility, and that is why modern rationalism is at an impasse. Edith wrote, "Through this means it is impossible to escape from the sphere of immanence to return to the objectivity from which Husserl started out and which he recognized the necessity of protecting. It is impossible to return to a truth and a reality void of all subjective reality." Never will "the mind in search of truth" be able to consent to "identifying existence with an automanifestative process of the consciousness." Also, one "makes God himself a relative something," and this is the most glaring difference between phenomenology as Edith knew it and Catholic philosophy. The first is "egocentric," the second "theocentric."[2]

In Husserl's work Edith understood the *projection* of the human being beyond his exclusive, individual "egocentric" world: she interpreted him correctly. But it was Husserl (a study easily enough bears this out and it is an almost incontrovertible fact) who receded into a renewal of subjectivisim. Edith went her own way and surpassed her teacher, going so far as to show how thomism, the most traditional philosophy of the Church—designated by Leo XIII, Pius X and Pius XII as the natural philosophy of Christianity—answers the questions that the most "modern" minds have expressed in phenomenology and existentialism.

The philosophy of St. Thomas avoids getting ensnared in the endless debate between post-Cartesian rationalism and idealism, by initially positing a foundation for intellectual knowledge in experimental perception through the senses. The first step for the human mind is to accept a real existing world outside itself. It recognizes that beings actually exist, that they are permanent and that our senses, though they do not reveal the essence of the world to us, at least do not deceive us in what they impart about the world outside the mind. In this way, we conclude that there really is a table here, that a solid is a solid, that a form remains the same as long as other internal or external forces do not change it, etc.

Childish? Perhaps it may seem so at first glance. But acceptance of these points is the only way to get out of the mind and into the world. It is the only way to escape the snags of solipsism, the only way to end up with having something *to think* about, reason about and act upon.

Phenomenology used a word found in medieval Christian philosophy and sneered at by nineteenth-century rationalism: *intentionality*. How does the mind grasp what it comes into contact with? How can we assimilate and assume something experienced in the world outside the mind? How can we distinguish order in the midst of chaos? We do not pause to think about such things because we are accustomed—too accustomed—to accept the "operations" of the mind and the "information" it gives us. Yet this is one of the greatest mysteries: the primary and basic correspondence between the forms of the world and the workings of the mind through which the intellect "captures" existence. In the mind's attention there is a profound *intention* that corresponds to what the world offers it to interpret.

The meaning of *intentionality* has been much discussed among phenomenologists and thomists, and we shall not go into it here. Let it suffice to say that from the time she began to examine St. Thomas and found the intellectual atmosphere she had been searching for, Edith Stein conceived of the intentionality of the mind in the way St. Thomas did.

However, on another point Edith's starting position in philosophy was not quite orthodox. She first wrote that the foundation and departure point for thomistic philosophy was faith. In reality, it was a natural experience—her encounter with the world—for Edith Stein. She set Husserl's idea that "the unifying point of departure is the transcendentally purified consciousness" in opposition to St. Thomas' "God and His Relation to Creation." Soon she came to see that the true thomistic foundation for knowledge is the relationship between creatures, and that it follows that the mind is made to know, since it comes into contact with creation; this results in a thorough knowledge of these creatures and their universe. The intellect perceives the necessity of a God and Creator.

Again, let us not be surprised at the direction of her thought. Faith revealed to her the meaning of the universe, and in a sense it was only natural for her to make faith the cornerstone and assign it the primary place in her intellect as she did in her life.

The progression of Edith's thought is extremely interesting. As far as she was concerned, there was not— and never could be—on the one hand, a philosopher who continued to think according to the laws of philosophy and, on the other, a person led to conversion by experiences from life and meditation on beings and their spiritual significance. Everything met and fused in her soul, and her mind was indissolubly bound to her soul. Her intellect moved her soul. As a philosopher, she perceived the imperfection of the world and saw the necessity for a Being more existent than all creation, which is but a manifestation of this Being. Hers was truly a *philosophical* conversion, the conversion of a *philosophical mind* that advanced from the first stages to the realization that for one to be fully a human being, one's mind and soul must be inseparable. Is it too much to say that this is her own message that Providence entrusted to her in the age of phenomenologists and existentialists?

She was born to ride the waves of existential phenomenology and draw inferences from it; to show from the failure of the best philosophies of the age—rationalism and idealism—that one must begin with the primary truths of the existence of an exterior world and the ability of the mind to know this world exterior to itself. She resolved these conclusions to their ultimate consequences. Philosophy can only lead to metaphysics, to the knowledge of being, to ontology. And ontology can only lead to God. No knowledge of being has failed to discover in the center of the world what Edith discovered there.

Chapter 5

The Way of Complete Surrender

Edith lived a voluntary monastic life at the convent in Speyer. The radiance of her interior life drew people's attention, and they came to her for advice and consolation. Edith's formerly rather distant personality gave way to a warm tenderness that let her become one with others in their trials. She was able to suffer with them and help them as only the saints, whose lives center on Christ, are capable of doing. "She gave solace to souls whom priests and spiritual directors considered lost."[1]

Her students, philosophy, spiritual guidance and most of all, prayer, were quite enough to keep her constantly active, but deep within her soul Edith wanted to give herself entirely to the contemplation of the Lord who had called her. Father Przywara, waiting for the moment when he was sure of her vocation (the Church is indeed wise), advised Edith to make several retreats with the Benedictines at Beuron.

Edith had been spending her summer vacations at home with her mother. She continued to be the same attentive, loving and beloved daughter. But a barrier was growing between mother and daughter—a chasm all the more insurmountable in that they loved each other and wanted to either win over or at least come to understand one another. On top of this, Edith lived in the midst of her entire intensely Jewish family, who did not understand her motives. When she tried to explain these motives to even her best friends, they hesitated to follow her for countless reasons—sometimes just to keep peace in their own families. The atmosphere stifled Edith. Beuron would surely be doubly a harbor of peace.

Father Przywara was making his own plans for Edith's future. Of late, Edith had taken interest in the German feminist movement. Why not get her to devote some of her intelligence and apostolic zeal to the Catholic Women's project? And so, in 1928, Edith launched into a new activity that began with a conference to the Catholic women teachers of Bavaria—a series of talks about the Church's views on woman's role in life.[2]

By now Edith was familiar enough with the thomistic approach to strike right at the heart of the problem with: "Is there a woman's nature?" Before knowing how to educate "the woman," or deciding what kind of life she ought to live, one must know what "woman" really is. Edith Stein then noted that one's actions cannot be considered separate from one's soul. Now a woman is meant by her very nature to be wife and mother, so no education can prescind from this vocation. "It is not her body alone that has a different structure," Edith affirmed, "and not only are there various individual physiological functions, but her whole physical make-up is different. There are different relations between a woman's body and soul, different connections between mind and sensibility...." Because she is as though *made for another* by her very essence, a woman "will find her strength in the intuition of the concrete and the living"; she is called to "grasp the concrete in its particularity."

Between 1918 and 1935 Germany reeled under the impact of internal disorder: the collapse of the post-bismarckian empire, the revolutions from 1918 to 1920; the economic chaos and unemployment crises. These not only upset the nation's political stability, but wreaked havoc on German family unity as well. Abruptly and brutally, Germany passed from the dominant Prussian Protestant Puritanism that the Wilhelmian government had inculcated into the fiber of the empire, to an erotic anti-moral anarchy, which, though it did not directly influence every family, gave rise to many formidable problems and challenged the accepted laws of moral living.

Amidst this disarray of thinking, Edith voiced more than the Church's tradition, for in a sense that was only secondary to her. Edith was first and foremost a young Jewish professor immersed in the activity of youth. She went on many of the long nature-outings that so deeply characterized this generation of the *Wandervögel*. She belonged to this generation and was herself a "bird-of-passage" in her questioning of all her era's ideas and lifestyles. Moreover, she was acquainted with the psychology of her times. It was her first specialty. She understood psychoanalysis and all the schools of scientific and experimental psychology.

Her conferences took her throughout the various colorful regions of Germany. Because of her immense background, Edith brought the girls and women who listened to her not the mouthings of a classic wisdom, but the discoveries of intellectual experience and the answers that modern psychology had to offer.

Edith's investigations taught her a great deal more than woman's subordination to man, and she denounced as a "deprivation proper to women" the concept of a life bound to man "by fetters of servitude" and "the wilting of a woman's mind in the physico-sensual life." Some of her works on "subordination to sex" are strikingly rel-

evant in the light of eroticism. No woman, she maintained, will find herself by simply being a "rebel slave." If
it be true that "the meaning of specifically womanly
existence cannot be understood merely in terms of relationships between men and women," and if the role of
the mother is essential, still neither of these relationships
helps us to fully understand all that a woman is. A
woman is no more meant *for* man than for herself. They
both have a place in God's plan.

In May of that year Edith was compelled to show "the
purpose of woman's formation." Just as there is an "imitation of Christ" for all humankind, so too there would be
an "imitation of Mary" for women.

We must not for a moment think that Edith lived in the
rarified atmosphere of abstract ideas. Quite the contrary,
she gleaned lessons that she could apply to the most
concrete facets of life, especially when she evolved an
ethic of feminine professions. And because she had thoroughly examined the "womanly type" confined between
the limits of Eve's sin and Mary's virginity, she dealt
with the most concrete of beings. What unity between the
loftiest and simplest we find here: "The inclinations of a
woman for what is living and personal" can be led "in the
wrong direction": "to desire to spend all her time exces-
sively on herself and others" or "taking too much interest
in others through sheer curiosity and indiscreet prying
into their lives."

With her writings on contemplation, Edith revealed
her inmost self. Try as she might not to rely on her own
experience, she betrayed with her very words the secrets
of her contemplative life. This is to be expected, for con-
stant attendance in choir, long hours of meditation before
the Eucharist, and unending prayer cannot but reveal
themselves.

"Losing oneself completely in a loving surrender to

God, allowing one's own life to come to an end to make room for God's life, is the motive and principle of the religious life." And Edith enumerated forms of love— love springing from compassion, protection, love rising out of participation (which "mourns with those who are mourning and rejoices with those who are joyful"). All these loves are "at the disposal of every creature so that it might become what the Father desires it should." In the heart of such a love, a woman's vocation is revealed: "to surrender oneself to another through love, to become entirely the property of another and to possess this other wholly—this is the deepest longing of a woman's heart."

Who, then, could "receive the surrender, the oblation, of a creature in such a way that its soul will not be lost, but saved?" Who, but God? And who "can abandon himself to us, filling our whole being by doing so, without losing anything of himself?" Who, but God?

Neither a woman's vocation nor her love are wholly realized except in the total giving of herself to God: "Complete surrender, the aim of religious life, is at the same time the only adequate fulfillment of a woman's aspirations."

Not all women have to enter the strictly religious life, but they must "in every way become the handmaids of the Lord, after the example of the Mother of God." When she spoke to the women of Germany, Edith never once hesitated to mention details of daily life to show the way great love is expressed in the observance of little things. She saw—and admired—her mother's life and it remained a blessed example for her to follow.

All Edith's attention was focused on her ideals. To keep them alive within her, she looked to the saints for examples to follow. She was especially fond of Elizabeth of Hungary. Elizabeth knew all the joy and fulfillment of great love. She could bask in the glory of her throne and a glittering reign. Yet in the midst of all that happiness and fame, her first concern was for the downtrodden, the starving, and all those whom the nobles at court wanted her to ignore. She wanted to do more for the God she loved, and she accepted the will of God when he took her husband during the Crusades. She forsook her wealth and consecrated herself entirely to the Lord by becoming one of his poorest servants when she openly adopted the Rule of St. Francis that she had long followed secretly.[3]

What more shining example than this? Edith Stein called upon her listeners to outdo the wonders of the saints themselves. The very source of light glows behind all their brilliant deeds. Among her conferences on St. Elizabeth of Hungary, there is one page in particular which best explains where the philosopher of Breslau had been heading for quite some time. She depicted Elizabeth as animated by love and pursuit of the Lord. "When her relatives allowed her to go about as she pleased, the Lord went with her, even into distant and strange lands. Because she knew he dwelt in the castle's chapel, she felt drawn to that place.... There she felt at home.... No one is as faithful as he." Such accents do not err. Elizabeth was much like the great St. Teresa, and Edith was like them both, wholly magnetized, entirely drawn toward him, seeing that the world of color is but a reflection of him and having no joy and peace except when in his presence.

Even then, Edith fully possessed her religious vocation, but the road to Carmel was closed to her. Dom Walzer, the Benedictine whose advice she sought during her retreats at Beuron Abbey, and Father Przywara as well, kept her in the world. Who was more qualified than Edith, an eminent philosopher and Jewish convert, to speak as she was to the women of Germany? That was her vocation. When she spoke of Elizabeth of Hungary,

the routine of daily living, or the primary duty of obedi-
ence, she spoke from actual experience. True, the road to
Carmel was still closed to her, but she had found the very
heart of existence, where knowledge and the soul are
intimately united. She had found the relationship between the natural and the supernatural and knew that
nature is not totally itself if it gives itself entirely to the
"natural" without being nourished by the supernatural,
to which one's deepest being is attracted.

We cannot discuss everything she taught about the
religious formation of children. This is a most important
topic because it is rooted in concise philosophical insight
and the thomistic vision of the human condition. "Faith is
not imagination," she wrote. "It is an intellectual appre-
hension. A fully developed faith is one of the most profound acts of the personality.... The emotions are certainly valuable aids and stimulating forces urging the
will to assent, but if the intellect and will are not called
upon to produce the greater part of the effort, one will
not develop a life of genuine and full faith."

Based on the loftiest philosophical and theological
grounds, Edith's vision of creation permitted her to give
those attending her conferences a way to avoid momen-
tary trends, without becoming oblivious to the needs of
the age. She could advance right to the center of the
problem, because she gauged its depth with the measur-
ing rod of doctrine: "The gentle weapons of psychology
and aesthetics are pledged to fight to the finish against
the real forces of temptation and passion. Only the fully
developed power of the Mystery can achieve victory on
this front." Edith also stressed: "A good part of Christian
formation consists in learning to lead one's life in communion with the Lord." One must "strike up the flames
of enthusiasm in one's heart" for the ideal that makes a
woman's life "the symbol of the mysterious union that

Christ contracted with his Church and with redeemed humanity."

This most modern of psychological technicians is truly an excellent example for us to follow. She in no way disdained the methods and means that psychology puts at our disposal to help people regain control of themselves and advance to God. But, because she was also an experienced philosopher and because she was becoming more and more a theologian, she knew, as she said herself, that human nature is not sufficient unto itself. Only the total spiritual life can come face to face with the problems of nature. Unlike many, Edith saw how impossible it was to first give children what is called "human" education and to wait until the "age of reason" before bringing divine life into their souls. As an experienced psychologist, she knew that the human being is fully human from the moment of conception until death. The qualities of imagination, sentiment, emotion and reason are not less present to the human person—at least potentially—right from conception, even though they awaken only slowly. She knew, as she taught, that the "divine force living within us" must nourish the whole being at every moment—and that one must have recourse to this power even in professional life.

How she would have liked to give herself up entirely to this force and divine presence! Already devoted to it, she lived a semi-conventual life at Speyer and made retreats and visits to Beuron. That same force guided her during her lecturing career. She aspired to more, but her spiritual directors did not recommend it. Faithful to them, she obeyed. Because they felt she would be more useful and influential, Edith sadly consented to resign from the staff of the private boarding school at Speyer on Easter, 1931, so as to seek a chair of philosophy at the University of Freiburg.

That year she spent almost the whole summer with her mother at Breslau. The atmosphere was oppressive. Her sister Rosa wanted to be baptized, but neither of them dared break their aged mother's heart again. Edith, who never ceased praying for her mother, hesitated, but her presence in Breslau helped to bolster Rosa up. For the time, at least, their mutual love for their mother made them spare her fresh heartaches.

No answer came from Freiburg and Edith applied for another position, whereupon she was offered a professorship in philosophy at Breslau. Frau Stein did not flinch at the sight of her daughter teaching Catholic philosophy in the city of her birth. She needed Edith with her, now more than ever. Edith's great love broke down the barriers.

During these months without work, Edith wrote a long tract on St. Thomas' writings on potency and act. She carried on a voluminous correspondence and answered all who came to her for help and advice. Their numbers constantly swelled—women who had attended her conferences, former pupils. She led them to the Psalms, advising them by means of the sacred texts.

At Breslau, she felt the lack of liturgical life: "The silent liturgy is my lot here. We can, of course, receive as much of this as we need, but it is only when I shall again live the liturgy in all its fullness that I shall feel how much of it I have been deprived of. When I left Speyer, I knew it would be quite difficult to live outside the cloister, but I had no idea how difficult." Who could still hold Edith back from what she was called to?

Her plans at Breslau did not materialize. In the spring of 1932, Edith accepted the lectureship at the Institute of Educational Theory at Münster. There, she could divide her time between feminine pedagogy and philosophy. During these years, Edith read Gertrude von Le Fort's book *The Song at the Scaffold*, which influenced Bernanos to write his *Dialogues des Carmelites.* She waited for her destiny to unfold into total prayer and sacrifice. Though it was not yet the proper time, she set out on the last lap of her journey, already in the unitive way of prayer.

Chapter 6

Edith's Prayer During the Gathering Storm

"She spoke little, but all her words were filled with meaning, for they sprang from the depths of silence and prayer," wrote a companion of Edith Stein.[1] She added, "How can one ever forget the sober glances, unspeakably sad, that she cast upon the Crucified, the King of the Jews, when she saw the constantly increasing threat of more violent racial persecutions? One day, I heard her say, 'Oh, how much my people must suffer before they become converted!' And the thought flashed through my mind that Edith was offering herself up to God for the conversion of Israel."

There is no reliable testimony or writing to tell us that Edith really was "offering herself up" for her Hebrew brothers and sisters, but we are inclined to think that Edith's piety had not yet taken so clearly defined a course. She was aspiring to the union of her whole being with the Lord and it was, indeed, a total offering that she had attained: an offering *already* realized, she was *sacrificed,* totally, sacrificed without stint, offered up in so intense a union with the divine will that her sacrifice was fully *made* for all. We may readily believe that, in her life of union in contemplative prayer, Edith had had the suffering of her people often before the eyes of her soul. To her own offering she united all the misery about to befall her people and brought it to him whom she loved; for, at the very root of everything about her, even her prayer, love governed all.

The text we quoted from Sister Aldegonde notes the two opposite poles around which Edith's life would revolve: prayer and suffering for her Jewish brethren, and the persecutions of Hitler that would swallow her up and bring her to her death.

Already, the expressions of her personal devotion had taken shape. The woman who remained so long motionless before the Eucharist waited for the grace she already possessed, whose presence she wished to make increasingly more welcome. Her prayer and devotion were, above all, responsive to grace. Was there anything more in addition to this?

Among the papers written during the period that she taught at Münster, Edith called people to more of a "general disposition" than to the development of "precise qualities." "We cannot acquire this condition by an effort of our own will; it must be the workings of grace. But we can and must open ourselves to grace." How? "By denying our own will completely and surrendering only to the will of God, making our whole soul receptive to recasting in his divine hands. Thus, silence and self-forgetfulness are bound together." She was not yet a Carmelite when she spoke these words, but hers was the spirit of St. John of the Cross and St. Teresa of Avila. Edith sketched an outline for daily living: If we rush headlong, throwing ourselves into the duties and cares of the day, then we must stop and say to ourselves, " 'Wait! None of this must bother me now. The Mystery of Redemption is what matters here, and not myself. I am allowed to share in this Mystery, *to be cleansed by it and rejoice in it*. I am permitted to offer myself and all my actions and sufferings, together with the spotless Victim on the altar.' And when the Lord comes to me in Holy Communion, I may ask him like St. Teresa, 'What do you want of me, Lord?' *and after this silent dialogue, I shall do what he bids me....* Because my soul will have gone out of itself, it will be able to penetrate into the divine life. The Lord will have enkindled in me the fire of charity, compelling me to share this fire of love with others.... The soul will clearly see the next stretch of road ahead. It will not see very far, but when it has traveled that distance, a whole new horizon will open up before it."

What serene abandonment these words contain! How in keeping with the peaceful humility of this little way of simple abandon is the royal road of contemplation! Edith had entered into this "silent dialogue" some time before, and she did not have to look for the life of the soul she described, because it was her own.

Meanwhile, Germany flared up all around her.

The Weimar Republic tottered on unsteady ground. Unemployment, misery, humiliation and political passions heaped coals onto this fire, which the Nazis fanned into an inferno.

In the spring of 1932, when Edith accepted a tutorial position at the Institute of Educational Theory in Münster, Germany entered upon the chain of events that one year later would bring Hitler to power. On May 10, Marshal Hindenburg was elected President of the German Republic and on June 1, Von Papen formed the government. On the fourteenth of June, Von Papen introduced the measure taken by the government of the Catholic Chancellor, Bruning, dissolving Hitler's SS and SA troopers. On July 31, the elections gave Hitler an overwhelming majority in the Reichstag.

But Edith went her own way: "One must find peace....

Nothing must deter us from containing ourselves and from fleeing to the Lord. He is ever present." If in the evening we are dissatisfied with ourselves, "Let us take ourselves for what we are...that we shall be able to find repose in him."

We should really be mistaken if we assumed that while Edith was absorbed in her interior life she was indifferent to what was going on in the world. In one of her earlier works, she had spoken of the "experience of a vanquished people," stating that one who "would share in the immense and unfathomable suffering encircling this people, finds himself overwhelmed by it." The swelling wave of hatred was about to crash down upon *her* people, the Jewish people, the people of her mother, brothers and sisters. Edith was always one of these people. Dom Feuling relates that, when he was going to Montmartre with her and Koyré, whom she had met in Germany and who was sent to teach at the Sorbonne, he heard them speaking of the Jewish people as "we." Edith's conversion had not destroyed the bonds of solidarity that bound her to her people. Besides, how could she feel freed from them when she had witnessed Frau Stein's grief at her daughter's apostasy every time she returned to Breslau, especially during her long stay there the preceding year?

By no means did she live isolated from the world. Rather, when she prayed she felt all the more intensely united to those who suffered.

"She hid her interior life," said the director of the Educational Institute of Münster, where Edith spent the year of 1932. "One had to guess at it or discover it indirectly," but "one could almost feel it when watching her at prayer." The Abbot of Beuron, after affirming that "her interior life was simple and straightforward...a soul lifted up to the heights, wholly illumined," went on to say that the very "idea of affecting a pose" was utterly alien to

her. On the contrary, "she did not want extraordinary
graces or ecstasies.... She desired only to be with God, as
though her presence in a holy place (the abbey) assured
her of a proximity with the mysteries of faith she could
find nowhere else.... Just as her body was fixed in an
almost total state of immobility, so also her mind dwelt
peacefully in the loving contemplation of God, in the joy
of our Lord."

Edith longed for the day when she could enter the
Carmel. There, she would be joined continually in the
prayer of the Church: "It seemed," wrote the Abbot of
Beuron, "that the liturgy, austere in both its length and
brevity, had become her indispensable food." But here,
too, Edith would embark upon a path where even her
fondness for the spiritual would not be wholly satisfied,
for she would have the Office with the Benedictines in all
its fullness, but "souls such as hers, once seized by the
spirit of the absolute, can only embrace a more singular
form of religious life, because the desire quickened in her
by the inspiration of the Holy Spirit would always beg for
more."[2]

The events that followed were in the hands of Providence. On January 30, 1933, Hitler became Chancellor of
the Reich. On February 27, the Reichstag was burned.
Two days earlier, Edith had given her last lecture at the
Educational Institute of Münster. For some time previous
to this, she had had to curtail her activities by holding her
conferences outside the Institute, where she was observed.
One of her pupils did not bother to hide the fact that she
was a follower of Hitler and she openly displayed her
copy of *Mein Kampf.* Edith encouraged her students to
form anti-Nazi groups. Though the general Jewish boy-
cott was not decided upon until April, intolerance constantly increased in the teaching profession. The time
inevitably came when Edith could no longer teach.

Edith had foreseen the new trial coming, but we might ask ourselves whether this really was a trial. It freed her for Carmel. Her real trial came in seeing the unbridled hatred of human beings. It was unbearable for her to think of the new sufferings that had befallen her aged mother, her brothers, and her sisters in Breslau. It was insupportable for Edith to think that the world had scorned the word of God and rejected Christ's grace.

Edith spent her last Christmas "in the world" (1932) in an Ursuline convent. One of the religious reports: "On Christmas Eve she joined with us in singing Matins; then we went to rest for an hour until midnight. When I returned to the church I found her still kneeling motionless in the same position as when we had left her. She then sang the Office of Lauds with us. When I asked her later whether she had not been weary, her eyes lit up and she replied: 'How could one grow weary on this night?'"[3]

Two months before (in October), she had given her last conference for the Catholic Women's League at Aachen. There she learned "to what extent the world had become a stranger and how much it cost [her] to remain in touch with it." She added that at the same time she had understood that she must "appear quite strange to those who lead active lives in the world."

Everything around Edith seemed to direct her to her truest vocation, beyond the intellectual life, beyond solitary prayer, beyond even the liturgical prayer of the Church. All was leading her to the vocation that she hinted at in the final months of 1932, just before her entrance into the Carmel: "There is a vocation that consists in suffering with Christ and thus in his redemptive work. If we are united to the Lord, we are members of his Mystical Body. Christ continues to live and suffer in his members, and suffering endured in union with him becomes his, made efficacious and united to his great redemptive work. The essence of the religious life, especially the Carmelite life, is to intercede for sinners and cooperate in the redemption of the world by *voluntary and joyous* suffering."

When she would later leave the Cologne Carmel to take refuge in a Dutch Carmel, Edith wrote her "Memoirs," in which she recounted some of the external circumstances of her vocation. She gave them to her prioress as a "Christmas gift." In this account, she particularly recalled one evening during the Lent of 1933, when, returning late from a meeting of Catholic intellectuals, she made her way toward the college where she lived. It was after the closing of the gates. A teacher there recognized her and invited her to spend the night at his apartment. While his wife prepared a room for her, he told her what the American newspapers were publishing about the atrocities committed against the Jews in Germany. "Suddenly, it became clear to me that the hand of God lay heavily upon his people and that the destiny of his people was my own."

On Thursday of Holy Week, Edith set out—as she had for the past five years—for the Benedictine Abbey of Beuron, where she spent Holy Week and Easter. She planned to go to Rome to request that the Holy Father write an encyclical on the Jewish question, and before doing so she wanted to find out what the abbot, Dom Walzer, who was returning from Japan, thought of her idea. At this time, Edith was an Oblate of St. Benedict at Beuron Abbey. On her way, she stopped at Cologne and prayed in the chapel of the Carmel. "I spoke interiorly to our Lord," she wrote, "telling him that I *knew* it was his cross weighing down upon our people. Most Jews did not recognize the Savior, but was it not the lot of those who did know him to bear his cross? That is what I want to do. I asked him only to show me how. And when the ceremony in the chapel finished (Vigil of the First Friday of the month), I became certain that he had answered my prayer. I did not know then what his cross would be for me."

The following day, Edith went on to Beuron, where the father abbot advised her not to go to Rome, since on his return trip he had seen the conditions there. When she arrived back at Münster, Edith learned that the officials had demanded that "Doctor Stein" quit teaching. Now nothing prevented her entrance into Carmel, since she could no longer have any influence in the world. The reason for remaining in the world was at last gone.

"For almost twelve years, Carmel has been my one goal, from the first day back in 1921 when the *Life* of St. Teresa fell into my hands and brought my long search for the true faith to an end. On New Year's Day, 1922, when I was baptized, I thought it but one more preparation for my entering the order of Carmelite Nuns." But at the express request of her spiritual advisors and because of the grief she would necessarily have brought to her mother, she had not entered the religious life. "Waiting had become very difficult for me," she wrote. "I had become a stranger in the world."

On April 30—Good Shepherd Sunday—after the Benediction of the Blessed Sacrament, she "received, inwardly, the Good Shepherd's consent," and that evening she wrote of her resolution to the Abbot of Beuron.

In May, Edith made contact with the Carmel of Cologne, which was just preparing a new foundation in Breslau, the city of Edith's birth. Received by the prioress, the sub-prioress and the novice mistress, she told them of her spiritual journey: "It always seemed that the Lord was keeping something for me in the Carmel that I could find only there."

On June 18 and 19, she returned from Münster to the

Carmel of Cologne, underwent the scrutiny of the chapter nuns and sang before them at their request: "It was harder for me than if I had delivered an address to a thousand people." On the following day, Edith received a telegram confirming her acceptance into the Carmel and giving her permission to live there for one month as a "guest," beginning on July 15. "Six huge cases of books preceded me to Cologne.... The month passed outside the "enclosure" (of the Carmel) was one of great happiness. I observed the sisters' Rule, working during my free time. I often visited Mother Josepha (the prioress) in the parlor and asked her any questions that happened to cross my mind. Her answers were always those I felt I would have given myself, and this agreement made me very happy."

On August 10, Edith went to Trier to receive the blessing of the abbot of Beuron. She spent the feast of the Assumption at the Abbey of Maria-Laach and then went on to Breslau.

Chapter 7

The Haven of Carmel

Edith told her family that the sisters of the Cologne Carmel had decided to accept her, but they thought this meant that she would be going to a new teaching post in October. Edith's sister Rosa met her at the Breslau station and Edith confided her plans to her. Rosa put off joining the Church in order to spare her mother any additional pain.

Frau Stein had weathered practically everything, but now she was struggling in vain against trials that came to her from all sides. When Jews were officially barred from all public offices, who would dare buy wood from Jews or even sell it to them?

Writing to a friend whom she especially asked to pray for her mother, Edith concluded with: "In the deepest security: *in tabernaculo Domini.*" The suffering ahead would not only be hers, but her mother's as well, and Edith loved her mother more than anyone else in the world, except the Lord. Edith had to cause this grief because of the summons she could not but answer—a most necessary obligation arising from the immense love that had taken hold of her entire life. This was the logical conclusion of her intellect, which was entirely dedicated to her Lord. There was no way out for her, driven as she was by love and fidelity to the truth. She had to add one more grief to all Frau Stein's other sufferings at the very time when the elderly widow's world was crumbling in about her and the foundations of the house she had so zealously built were collapsing beneath her.

Edith's love for the persecuted Jews necessitated that final step, for if she were to raise up to the Lord a prayer sprung from a Jewish heart and if she were really to suffer the lot of the Jewish people, she believed that she absolutely had to enter Carmel, even at the risk of breaking her mother's heart. Abraham's sacrifice was realized in Edith's oblation, in blood and tears.

"My mother suffered intensely from the political turn of events," wrote Edith in her "Memoirs" to the prioress. "She was continually upset over the problems caused by 'those evil men' (the Nazis and their henchmen)." Heaped on top of this agitation was an additional personal loss: Erna, now a doctor, had moved to another section of Breslau and had taken her family with her. "Erna and her husband and children were a joy and consolation for Mother. She bitterly resented their leaving."

Frau Stein "seemed to come to life again" with Edith's arrival: "When she came home from work in the evening, she enjoyed sitting down and knitting close by the desk where I worked. She would tell me everything that had happened to her that day.... I got her to tell me about the past.... My presence did a great deal for her. But I thought to myself: "If you only knew....""

The dreaded day finally arrived when Frau Stein asked, "What are you going to do with the sisters at Cologne?" Edith answered, "Live with them." Immediately there followed a "desperate attempt" to dissuade her, after which Edith felt that "a great wall had come between the two of us." She added, "There was no peace from that day on." After Frau Stein had exhausted herself with these "angry outbursts," she succumbed to long "periods of silent despair."

"I had to take the step alone and wholly plunged into the darkness of faith," Edith wrote. No one around her understood. Her entrance into the convent at the very moment when the Jews were suffering bitter persecution seemed a betrayal and desertion of her people. But she remained firm in the knowledge that she had decided to give herself completely to the Lord so that he might shower his grace upon the Jewish people, take pity on them, comfort them in their suffering, and lead those who recognized him into the Church.

Edith set out for Cologne on October 12, the Day of Atonement, one of the greatest Jewish feasts, and her birthday as well. On the morning before she left, Edith went to the synagogue with her mother and they walked home afterwards. Edith tried to ease her mother's inner grief by stressing that these first months at the Carmel were only a period of trial. But Frau Stein knew her daughter. "If you have decided to try out this life, it is because you intend to persevere in it." Then she discussed the rabbi's sermon. Edith acknowledged that one could be devout in Judaism, "if one has not learned anything beyond that." Frau Stein said, without calling Christ by name, "I have nothing against him. He may well have been a good man. But why did he have to make himself God?" At that instant, the discussion between mother and daughter touched the very heart of the Jewish spiritual drama.

Danielou mentions in his book, *Scandaleuse Vérité*, that a rabbi once told him, "'You see, we Jews reproach Christ because he tried to change the Law. God gave us the Law, and God alone can change what he has given.'

"I said to him," continues Danielou, "'You could tell me nothing that would please me more. The Law was given by God; God alone can change what he has given; therefore, if Jesus thought he had the right to change the Law, it was because he thought he was God.' "

The agony of Edith's departure was softened by an act of great tenderness. Sitting down, the elderly woman— eighty-four years old—"buried her face in her hands" and wept. Edith went up behind her chair and "pressed her poor, dear wizened head to my heart.... We remained so for a long while, until it was time to go to bed. I took her to her room and for the first time in my life, helped her undress. Then I sat on her bed...until she told me to get some sleep. Neither of us slept that night."

Edith left the next morning, after one last loving embrace, and spent that night "in a profound peace" at the threshold of the house of the Lord, in the Carmel of Cologne.

In a testimony given about Edith, the Abbot of Beuron wrote that "she did not choose the little Carmel of Cologne in the hope of coming to live with a learned prioress and a group of highly educated nuns." At the Carmel "she was the only intellectual, and she soon became the least of the sisters there." She did not dream of asking permission to continue her philosophical work in the convent, nor did she authorize her friends to intervene on her behalf to the superiors of the Order to grant her that permission: "Her sole desire was to disappear, to lose herself in the Carmel." And since she was inept at manual labor, she came to rejoice in being one of the least of the servants and drew near to the very essence of humility. She learned humility when one religious saw her only as a sister who handled a broom quite badly. She learned humility when she admitted to the prioress that she had "a hard time learning all the little rules." But she had desired all this for so long.

The strict poverty of her cell symbolized silence toward every word except the Word of God, and she had always desired this kind of poverty. "There was no need at all to prepare her for the life of renunciation," wrote the Abbot of Beuron. "She entered the Carmel like a child rushing into its mother's arms, joyful and singing, without ever regretting the choice she had made."

Her new life was truly one of fulfillment, not of renunciation. The serenity and peace she had felt on the train going to Carmel may shock us, surely, when we consider that she had just left her mother in bitter anguish. But, because she knew that in entering into Catholic prayer she was not betraying her brethren in Israel, but instead was coming to serve them where they could best be served, so too, she knew that there she could best show how much she loved her mother by praying that Jesus might console her grief. Who, better than Jesus, knew the sufferings of a mother?

What looked like renunciation was really not. Her breaking away from home was not what it appeared to be, and her seeming departure *from* life was in reality her entrance *into* life. Once Edith wrote to a religious who sought her advice, "I believe that the response we must make is *Fiat voluntas tua*. The Holy Rule and the Constitutions are for us the expression of the divine will. Our participation in the sacrifice of Christ consists in sacrificing our personal inclinations to them. Furthermore, charity demands that we adapt ourselves to the customs of the house and the tastes of the community. *If we do it to gladden the heart of Jesus, it will not be a constraint for us, but rather the exercise of freedom in what is more noble, a voluntary act of love toward our Bridegroom.*"

Edith continually radiated joy. She would tell the prioress that she had never laughed so much as in the recreation periods at the Carmel. Hers was a spiritual joy rising out of her union with God. It was also the childlike

and carefree joy of a nature freed from extra burdens of
its own making. But in the midst of this new life there
was a sharp thorn that drove her to intense prayers of
supplication: every Friday Edith wrote to her mother, but
she never answered.

Edith did find some difficulty in adapting to community life. Her ineptitude at manual labor was a unique
cross. She told Frau Conrad-Martius how difficult it was
to get used to "all the little details of the religious life."
But even these difficulties became part of her joy; they
were like the "small change" of the immense treasure
that she offered the Lord and that he redeemed in joy.
What counted was the essence of this life that she had so
long desired, hoped for and awaited—the total oblation
of herself to him whom she loved, a lasting presence with
him, total absorption in him and therefore, always greater
nearness to him. How could Edith help but be joyful?
And when news came from the outside, how could she
not but offer these heartaches as a pledge of her love for
her Lover?

On Sunday, April 15, 1934, Edith received the Carmelite
habit: hempen sandals, a fifteen-decade rosary, the long
brown robe. But first, before she could wear these, she
donned a white satin wedding dress. April 15, Good
Shepherd Sunday, was the anniversary of the day she
had asked God to let her enter the Carmel.

A few days later, Hitler would set up the Popular
Tribunal in Berlin. On the first of May he was to organize
the Ministry of Science, Education and Popular Culture,
which would permit the pretentious nonsense of Rosen-
berg to become the philosophy of a whole people. Through
these actions the Nazis would persecute Jews and Catholics all the more. But Edith was completely absorbed in
her interior joy.

Clothed in her wedding dress, Edith walked out of the

cloister to greet her old friends and all who could come to
see her: the Abbot of Beuron, who celebrated the High
Mass, the father provincial of the Carmelite Order, her
godmother Conrad-Martius and a group of friends and
students. Doctor Stein would henceforth be only Sister
Benedicta. She had chosen this name to signify her grati-
tude to God and her high esteem for the great founder of
Western monasticism.

At the sound of the bells, Edith was led up to the altar,
where white flowers greeted her from all sides—gifts
from her former pupils, the Catholic Women's Associa-
tions and her university friends.

"What do you seek?"

"The mercy of God, the poverty of the Order and the
company of the sisters."

"Are you thus resolved to persevere until death?"

"Thus do I hope and desire, relying on the mercy of
God and the prayer of the sisters."

The sisters opened the cloister: Edith entered, carrying
a lighted candle in her hand. Before her, the Carmelites,
also holding candles, formed the welcoming community
that Edith was about to enter—the community of continual prayer, of an ardent fire of love that will never
cease being expressed. Edith kissed the crucifix they held
out to her. With the prioress leading her by the hand,
Edith, now vested in the brown robe, returned from the
grille and received the blessed scapular and cincture that
she could never refer to as "her own": "Receive the sweet
yoke of Christ and his burden that is light.... When you
will become old, another will gird you...."

Arms outstretched in the shape of a cross, Edith pros-
trated herself on the chapel floor. The *Veni Creator* was
intoned:

"Best of comforters,
delightful and refreshing guest of the
        soul,
rest in toil, refreshment in the heat of
day, solace in grief,
O most blessed light,
fill the hearts of your faithful....
Grant to those who trust in you
The sevenfold gift of grace...."

Edith gave the kiss of peace to her new sisters:
"How very good and pleasant it is
when kindred live in unity!...
It is like the dew of Hermon,
    which falls on the mountains of Zion."

                                      (Psalm 133)

Sister Benedicta now began to follow in the footsteps of Teresa; the oblation had been offered, never to be taken back.

Yes, she had made the total gift of herself. The father provincial of the Carmelites knew how much was concealed in this *total* gift. And scarcely had Sister Benedicta entered the cloister than he asked her to take up intellectual work once again. In the Carmel, Edith was to write her most beautiful works: *The Mystery of Christmas, Eternal and Infinite Being, The Science of the Cross, Hymns to the Church.*

Edith placed herself into "the hands of the Infant," the hands that "take and give at the same time," the hands that "take the wisdom of the wise, who become as guileless as infants," for "before the Infant, in the manger, their minds are laid bare."

Does she not speak of her own experience in these words? "In the kindergarten of the spiritual life, when we begin to walk and let ourselves be led by God, we feel his presence very strongly. His hand holds us...." But the "dark night" comes "that steals over the soul when the divine light no longer shines.... God is always there, but he is hidden and he keeps silent." Why? "These are the mysteries of God that we touch upon and they cannot easily be understood." But "God became man to let us share in his divine life: that is the beginning and the final goal." To have this "share," this participation, "everyone must suffer and die," must "participate fully" and consent to the darkness of the dark night, because this "torment" is permitted by God "to compensate for the sins of another.... That is why we must say: May your will be done, especially in this dark night of the soul...." Because our suffering, even the suffering of the "dark night," is joined to the suffering of Jesus, it is also joined to the redemption. Christmas Eve recalls to our minds the beginning of this ascent that we must make.

We have seen the central light that Edith found for her life and which drew her to the Carmel; we have seen it spring first from her research and philosophical meditations. Because she had pursued Husserl's ideas further than he had himself, seeking to determine the one thing consistent in the existence of the universe, she had gone beyond the universe of things and entered into that creation which gave the universe its existence and meaning. The light she discovered not only brightened her life, but also resolved her philosophical problems. Because she found the light of existence, she came to see in her philosophical work that the mind aided the soul in finding itself. Now that her soul enlightened her mind, her intellect reached out to love. Love guided her intellect from then on.

Edith read Heidegger's *Being and Time*. She knew the author and was interested in this new thinking. Formed by Husserl and her contact with Heidegger, she was well versed in the thought that made up the existentialist current. This explains the one ground for complaint that we have—her confusion between philosophy, which begins with experience and reason, and theology, which uses reason to better understand what has been learned through revelation. The characteristic mark of phenomenology and existentialism is the rejection of such distinctions in order to concentrate on the flux of being, so as to glean its most profound significance. Edith continued on this road, constantly clarifying her philosophical research, guided by the light of revelation which gives the ultimate meanings behind the realities of the world that philosophy examines: the individual, nature and thought.

If we are to take *Eternal and Finite Being*[1] for what it is— that is, a book that thoroughly confuses theology and philosophy—at least let us be able to distinguish what was and what remains the touchstone of Edith's conversion. Here, conversion is understood in its literal meaning: *a turning toward,* a turning of the mind to what must satisfy it. For Edith Stein, the *ego* was seen as an undeniable reality. The ego is certain of existing, and of existing *in time,* for it sees itself as a "now" between a "nevermore" and a "not yet."

Thus, by experiencing the *being* that we are, we come to know of an existence that is to come (our future). We *are* and yet we are not *all* that we are (the completed, but subsistent, past; the future that draws us and already forms us by its very summoning). From this experience—while existentialism finally concludes that, if we are not what we are, it is because we are not—Edith Stein, on the contrary, concluded to what she called a being that is simple, a pure Being, with no admixture of non-being, and therefore permanent, eternal: God.

That was the *philosophical* path of Edith Stein: she concluded her first philosophical meditation and polished it off in a really *thomistic* style. But on the way, she did not neglect all the wealth of her existentialistic experience. She did not forget the analytic depth of Heidegger's dereliction: "This term expresses above all that man is found to exist without knowing how he came to be.... But the question of his origin is not done away with. However much one may try to ignore such a question...it will irresistibly arise from the singularity of the human being that demands a self-sufficient Being to be the cause of everything and to be the cause of himself—which requires him who moves what is moved."

She followed Heidegger—and preceded more than one French existentialist—in the analysis of anxiety. But she considered also that the human being encounters joy. Heidegger said that each of us is, as it were, "thrown into existence," and she forced this argument into a corner. Yes, we perceive ourselves as unavoidably participating in existence. But exactly because anxiety and the possibility of being reduced to total or partial nothingness hovers over us, we perceive at the same time the existence of what made us to be and sustains us in existence.[2] There is a Being more existent than ourselves, who himself possesses all the being he gives us. He gives meaning to the anxiety we feel when we imagine that we might cease existing.

Having arrived at this contemplation of the Being, Edith was no longer in the realm of philosophy. Her spiritual life entered the picture here, and when she perceived this divine Being as a Trinity, it was still the spiritual life speaking to her. Let us not be disappointed if in one place or another—the problem of evil, for example—Edith did not follow the traditional routes. It was an entirely different matter—the encounter of a soul with the divine Eternity.

Chapter 8

The Science of the Cross
Offering, Persecution, Exile and Death

Sister Teresa Benedicta of the Cross made her temporary vows on Easter Sunday, April 21, 1935. She was fully at home in her new life and her heart experienced a blissful serenity. Edith had slipped easily into the life of adoration and prayer she had so long desired and found her fulfillment in this life. Everyone who saw her as a Carmelite speaks of the peace and joy radiating from her. Gertrude von Le Fort,[1] who knew Edith while she lived in the world and later in the convent, describes her "radiant, almost transfigured countenance." A university friend used the same words in describing Edith: "Her happiness overwhelmed me." When asked whether she had become accustomed to the solitude, Edith answered, "I was more alone throughout most of my years in the world than I have ever been here." When a lady admired her saintliness, Edith replied, "We gladly share the peace of the convent with you, but you must never attribute to mere human beings what continues to be a pure gift of God."[2]

Dom Feuling saw her while she was in the cloister and judged her as "matured" both in her humanity and in her faith, "wholly spiritualized...she transcended the world," and "attained the barely perceptible degree of experimental knowledge that St. Thomas attributes to the gifts of the Holy Spirit.... A soul offered up, wholly given to God. If the great Teresa of Avila's primary purpose is to lead her daughters to the mystical life and union with God by means of contemplation, I dare say that Sister Benedicta walked firmly up this road...."[3]

Meanwhile, beyond the convent walls, Germany degenerated into that seething world of hatred and violence that Edith had foreseen and feared. She was not afraid for her own safety—the total oblation of herself could only be achieved by the sacrifice of her life—but for the safety of her loved ones: her mother, brothers, sisters, all "her people." A friend who described her joy in the religious life, told Edith how happy she was to see her safely behind the grille of Carmel. "Don't believe it," Edith retorted. "They will come after me even here. And in any event, I don't count on being spared."

In 1935, the year Edith took her temporary vows, Hitler legalized the Jewish persecutions. On September 15, at Nuremburg, Hitler spoke about the Jewish question, while promulgating the "law for the protection of German blood and honor," and the law was rigorously upheld that following December. Frau Stein, now in her eighty-eighth year, and her children became hunted outcasts with no rights or privileges whatsoever.

To see how well Edith accepted all these trials, we have only to flip through the pages of her *The Science of the Cross*,[4] which she wrote while at the Carmel. This book remained unpublished until 1950. First of all, Edith described the degrees of grace introduced by St. John of the Cross—whose work she followed—up to the penetration of the divine Mystery. She depicted the dark night of the soul, not symbolically, but as a spiritual reality into which the creature ascending toward God is plunged: "The night is invisible and shapeless. And yet we perceive it...closer to us than anything else. It has become an intimate part of us." The light makes things appear as they truly are, while the night enshrouds them, "threatening to swallow us up as well." What is in darkness is "invisible and formless...like a shadow or threatening specter."

Edith inversely depicted the obsession and perception of the Being who guided her to the Church and its traditional philosophy. In the light of these pages, one comes to understand how Edith the philosopher approached and finally entered the Church of Christ, which alone answered her problems about complete and full existence. The book illustrates how she confused her deductive philosophical work and her theology, which meditates on the experiences of the "other" given by revelation.

Our existence, then, is "inwardly, not outwardly, threatened by dangers lurking in this night." In Sartre's existential "annihilation" of man, the "dark night" of the mystics, Edith saw the only solution and knew its dramatic intensity. In the immediately apparent emptiness that exists in the world and in our hearts, certainly rational experience begins to bear witness to the truth of an existence acting on the world and revealing itself in relationships among persons. Existential "nothingness" may show up in the very heart of existence as the experience of the futility of things. The night, "depriving our senses, hampers our activity, paralyzes our faculties." This is a concise image of the night of the mind and soul, but it is much more than just an image, for this is an experience actually undergone by souls.

The "night" of the mystics is a language—God's language speaking and drawing souls ever nearer to him.

The mystical night, seen as *God's absence*, speaks of God and announces him. "There is a soft nocturnal glow in a mind that is freed...calmed and meditative before plunging into reality...." If this night is to be at all beneficial to the soul, the soul must consent to it and understand it as a test, a token of love awaiting love. A "night" forcing the soul to withdraw into itself by refusing love is despair. And this is the path taken by more than one existentialist, even before mystical experience. "If we agree to believe through faith,[5] and if we entirely accept Christ...he will guide us by his passion and cross" to the glory of the resurrection.... After the dark night has passed, the "Living Fire of Love" will "illumine the secret relationships between God and the soul.... In this way, the spiritual marriage between the soul and God, for which God created it in the first place, will be achieved and consummated on the cross and sealed with it for all eternity."

We cannot say—only the Church dares to say—precisely what Edith Stein's spiritual experience was. The light shed by some of her many letters of spiritual direction written at the Carmel, reveal the experience of a soul that found certitude in the joy of its love.

To one Dominican religious who asked whether mystical graces are reserved to special people, Edith replied, "The decisive factor is conformity to the divine will. John of the Cross and Teresa of Avila saw this to be essential. The surest way for us is to empty ourselves of everything, so that we can then be attentive to divine grace." This well defines Edith's own life. And from the inaccessible interior refuge which is anything but an escape, she looked the world squarely in the face and thought of the "priests and religious confined in prison," for whom "everything is grace" because they possess "God and the Trinity completely" within them.

We know how Edith came to the immense interior

peace that nothing could shake, not even the trials or dangers pressing upon her. We know how because she depicted it in *The Prayer of the Church*, which is certainly one of her finest works.

Prayer dwelt within her from the very beginning of her spiritual journey before her baptism. She recognized the two essential ideas of prayer. The first is: "The work of redemption is consummated in secret and in silence. The living prayers that help form the kingdom of God, the instruments he chooses to work with, are cut and honed in silent dialogue between souls and him." The second concept is that personal prayer, individual prayer and the prayer of the Church are one reality, one flowing stream: "The torrent of mystical graces running through the ages forms the source and deepest part of the stream of the Church's prayer, and there are no diverted branches of this stream."[6]

Edith knew and desired long encounters with the Lord, even before entering the Carmel. She understood that the mystical life and prayer were not separate, but that each supported and naturally engendered the other. She wanted and loved the Divine Office sung in common and she practiced it during her long contact with the Benedictine religious before entering the Carmelite Order. This experience helped her to better understand how there can be but one prayer and not individual or group prayer: "The Divine Office passes the news from one generation to the other.[7] A great many voices fade into one another and are lost as though swept away in the rushing torrent of the mystical stream whose booming sound rises up in a canticle of praise to the Holy Trinity, God, Creator, Redeemer and Life-giver. It is wrong to separate or to set in mutual opposition subjective personal prayer and objective social, liturgical prayer. Every true prayer is the prayer of the Church. Every prayer operates in the Church and the whole Church prays in every prayer, for the Holy Spirit dwells in it."[8] Is this not what Edith Stein felt going on within her?

Edith wanted to express all she saw in prayer and professed with every ounce of her being by putting the conclusion of the Eucharistic Prayer into a chapter heading of *The Prayer of the Church:* "Through him, with him, in him, in the unity of the Holy Spirit, all honor and glory is yours, almighty Father, for ever and ever."

Our personal reality and prayer and the Church's reality and prayer are not two distinct realities, two paths to God. We only have existence through participation in Him-Who-Is. We pray only when our prayer joins in with the great praise of everyone throughout the earth which alone validly expresses him in the sacrifice of the One in whom all prayer finds its source and meaning. Our prayer exists only because it is rooted in total offering and is one with that of the Church.

"Christ is the center of the universe. He offers himself for it and became man to renew it inwardly and bring it to perfection. He calls upon the whole of the created universe to give thanks to the creator in union with him."[9] Edith guessed at the "Eucharistic meaning of prayer" from the outset of her spiritual journey. She expressed it by citing a psalm:

"O Lord, I love the house in which you dwell,
and the place where your glory abides" (Ps 26:8).

This had led her to the foot of the altar long before she entered into the joy of the Carmel. She manifested this truth outwardly in her priestlike attitude before the altar. Some people considered her cold and distant because of this. One religious said that she "couldn't understand how one might stand so long before the Eucharist without tiring." This was Edith's personification of her total union with Christ.

Pray in order to be united, be united to pray—this is a double progression. One who prays is offered and asks to be joined with Christ's merits, requesting that one's suffering be made acceptable and asking the grace necessary for one's prayers to be received and united to the merits of the holy passion. As the action of God, liturgical prayer *acts* so that God might wait for us. It is also the action of God within us, transforming our being into what God waits for.

True, Jesus prayed alone, but he also prayed with the people, and he expects us to pray together, until at length "all may be one." "Where would soldiers be without their captain?" asked St. Teresa. Personal prayer is valid because it is united to the prayer of the Church and the communal Eucharist, which alone prefigures the Eternal Unity.

Though at the apex of the spiritual life, Edith never forgot the world. Neither did her great patron saint. Edith and Teresa both saw that the world is best served in the heart of prayer: "The Lord alone knows how much the prayer of St. Teresa and her daughters contributed to safeguard Spain from heresy. God alone knows what power they wielded during the bitter religious wars in France, the Low Countries and the Germanic Empire."

Because Edith saw this fact, she always preserved her deep interior peace and imperturbable, almost rash, serenity, while her loved ones sank beneath the oppressive Nazi tyranny.

During those frightful days, she wrote *The Science of the Cross*, and Providence prepared her for worse things to come.

After long sufferings, Frau Stein died on September 15, 1936. They tried to tell Edith that her mother had died a Christian, but she refused to believe them; she knew in her heart that her mother had died praying in the Jewish faith. Having waited until after her mother's death, Rosa received the sacrament of baptism and then rejoined her sister, who, by a fortunate accident, was in the hospital. There they could visit freely. It had happened that one night the prioress heard a delicate cough on the darkened staircase of the convent and went to investigate. There she found Edith, who had fallen in the darkness and broken her hand and foot. Edith had coughed because the Rule forbade any infraction of the grand silence.

Rosa was baptized on Christmas Eve.

The Carmel of Cologne began its preparations for the three-hundredth anniversary of its foundation. Edith did her share of the work and at the same time kept up a vast correspondence, giving spiritual direction to other religious, priests included.

On April 21, 1938, Edith took her final vows, while all about her the world seethed at the brink of war, vividly reminding her of why she was offering herself to God. Six days after her solemn profession Husserl died. Being non-Aryan, he had lost his professorship at Freiburg and had taken refuge in the convent of St. Lioba, where Edith had often gone to pray and which one of her own students entered after being converted. Husserl had something akin to a vision on Good Friday, seeing "light and darkness; a great darkness and, once again, the reappearance of light."

On April 10, 1938, ten days before Edith's profession, Germany's national elections gave the Nazi party ninety-nine percent control over the Reichstag. A month earlier Hitler had entered Vienna.

The religious had been obliged to vote in this election and Edith had urged them to vote against Hitler. On the morning of the balloting, several government officials brought a ballot-box into the convent parlor, so they would have no trouble in finding out just *how* the sisters voted. The prioress objected in vain; they had to cast their ballots immediately. The officials noticed that "Doctor Edith Stein" did not vote. The sisters told them that she was a "non-Aryan," whereupon one of them noted the "admission" in writing.[10]

Edith's brother and her sister Erna, with her children, left Germany before the persecutions got under way. In September of 1938, Hitler began his campaign to unite the Sudetenland to Germany and occupied the territory in October. On November 9, the pogroms broke out throughout the length and breadth of Germany. The Cologne synagogue was burned. Edith wrote, "The shadow of the cross has fallen over my people." It had also fallen over her.

Edith agreed to take refuge in Holland in the Echt Carmel, which had taken in the Carmelite refugees from Cologne during the *Kulturkampf*.[11]

She crossed the frontier on the foggy night of December 31 and the sisters of Echt welcomed her. Rosa would soon join her there.

On Passion Sunday (1939), Edith wrote to her superior for permission to "offer herself to the Sacred Heart of Jesus as a sacrifice of atonement for the peace of the world." She added, "If the reign of Antichrist could be shortened without another world war,...I should offer myself today, for it is the twelfth hour. I know I am nothing, but Jesus desires it, and he will undoubtedly ask it of many others."

In the midst of so many perils, the sisters of Echt admired her "cheerfulness." In a letter written to her friend, Hedwig Conrad-Martius, in November, 1940, Edith remembered to thank her godmother for "the many fine mirabelle plums" the convent owed to the excellent horticultural advice of Hans Conrad-Martius.

In the summer of 1940, Rosa in her turn crossed the

frontier and joined her sister. They were never again to be separated.

Now began the silence of prayer where death was more real than the turmoil of life. It is quite evident that during her final months on earth, Edith passed into the world in which St. John of the Cross had been utterly absorbed.[12] She wrote: "Our Father St. John understood *pure love* as the love of God for God himself, by a heart free from all attachment to created things, free from self and others, free even from all the consolation that God gives a soul—that is, *a heart which only desires the accomplishment of the will of God and is guided by him without the least resistance....* Must we try to attain this state of pure love? Most surely, for that is the purpose for which we have been created. It will be our eternal life, and we must come as close to it on earth as possible. Jesus is made man to be our life. What can we do? Struggle with all our might to become detached from all things.... Empty our minds of all natural curiosity by fixing on God the simple regard of our faith" (Letter of March 13, 1940). Edith surrendered wholly to such detachment.

On Sundays, Edith and Rosa visited in the parlor. Rosa had brought Edith news of the ominous turmoil wracking the world, especially the persecutions of Jews and Catholics. The nuns at Echt learned of the great upheaval in many ways, not the least of that was the engine throb of glutted bombers traversing the skies over the Carmel to destroy German and British cities.

Edith kept herself busy by writing the life of Sister Aimée de Jesus. She launched into the mystique of Psuedo-Dionysius and taught Latin to the novices: "They are excellent students and give me much joy. What a tremendous grace it is to have so many young people in our little family of sisters who are all somewhat up in years." Sometimes the "older" convent family seemed disconcerted by Edith's dispensation from all the community's manual labor so as to devote all her free time to study. They were upset, too, because Rosa's stories of the war and persecutions made them uneasy. They were afraid Edith would attract unfavorable attention to the convent. In the midst of all this, Edith abandoned herself to the "detachment" of St. John of the Cross.

The Carmelite who asked Christ to fill her with "emptiness" was not all blind or deaf to what was going on around her. She knew her desire to be offered for the Jewish people would soon be fulfilled. It was a grace that her offering had been accepted, but if she really *knew* of this acceptance, it could have been a grave cause of spiritual pride. Yet she continually offered herself for "others," the "others" with whom she lived, because the responsibility for sin is common, and still more, perhaps, because she wanted to help save "her Jewish people." "I think mostly of the responsibility we all share in others' guilt," she wrote when commenting on Psalm 19.[13]

"The others": the Jewish people, the Nazis...all "others," who were indifferent to the persecution, indifferent to love.... Beyond this, enduring it, she hoped and longed for the "emptiness" of fulfillment.

Edith felt the sun that had shone over her brief existence begin to set. Everything had been taken away from her—or rather, she had given all: her family, her two "nations," Germany and the Jewish People, her university life and her spiritual family at Cologne. She was alone in a new convent in a foreign land, with only Rosa—her sole tie to her former life—bringing news of hatred and persecutions from the world beyond the cloister. She still clung to the hope-filled "emptiness" of her father, John of the Cross: "The history of monastic souls is a marvelous one. They are deeply hidden away in the divine Heart. *And what we so often think we understand is but a pale reflection of what remains the mystery of God until the day when all will be revealed to us. My greatest joy is hope in the light to come.* "

While discussing Pseudo-Dionysius, she wrote, "The prophet has no need to see God with his eyes or his imagination and in spite of all evidence to the contrary, he has the interior certitude that God speaks to him." She employed the impersonal "one" where her own personal experience seemed to be speaking: "This certitude is perhaps founded on the feeling that God is present. One feels touched by him who is in the most intimate center of our being. This is, strictly speaking, what one calls the *experience of God,* essential to every mystical experience where one encounters God as one creature meets another."

For some time, the Carmel of Echt had planned to get Edith into a neutral country. The Swiss Carmel of Paquier agreed to accept her, but Edith could not leave without Rosa. Thinking back on it now, we might believe that they began negotiating for a Swiss passport too late. In any case, Edith and Rosa were called to Maestricht by the Gestapo. Upon entering the office, Edith saluted, not with the usual "Heil Hitler" but with the "Praised be Jesus Christ" of the convent. They were breaking the law by not wearing the yellow "Star of David" on their outer garments. Later they were summoned to the inquisitors of the Jewish Commission in Amsterdam. One officer told Edith about the bombing of Cologne and the destruction of Holy Mary of Peace, where Edith had paused to pray before crossing the frontier.

Several priests advised her to escape "illegally," but she refused to do this because she would not have her sisters suffer the consequences of her escape.

In July, 1942, the Dutch Catholic hierarchy solemnly protested against the Jewish persecutions. Soon after-

wards, Edith learned that her brother Paul and his family
had been taken to a concentration camp. Edith doubted
that she could secure a passport for Switzerland and
wrote: "I shall accept everything God wills.... For several
months I have worn over my heart a verse from the
Gospel of St. Matthew: 'When they persecute you in one
town, flee to the next; for truly I tell you, you will not
have gone through all the towns of Israel before the Son
of Man comes'" (Mt 10:23).

On August 2, in reprisal for the letter promulgated by
the Dutch hierarchy that had spoken out against the
persecution and which formally stated—against German
prohibitions—that Christians of Jewish origins could not
be deported, all Catholic "non-Aryans" in Holland were
arrested. At 5 o'clock in the evening, while the sisters
were in choir, the prioress was called to the parlor by two
German officers. Believing they had come to give her the
passports for Switzerland, she signaled for Edith. One of
the Germans ordered Edith to leave "in five minutes."
Edith replied, "I cannot. The Rule of cloister forbids it."

"Get this out of the way (the grille) and come out," the
officer demanded.

Edith replied calmly, "I must not leave."

The officer called the prioress. Edith returned to choir
to kneel before the Blessed Sacrament, while the prioress
argued with the officer.

"Sister Stein must leave the convent in five minutes."

"But the Stein sisters are waiting for their passports."

"That will be taken care of later. Give her a blanket and
three day's rations."

Rosa knelt before the cloister for the prioress' final
blessing. Edith came down from her cell, surrounded by
the sisters, and then the two of them left with the officers.
The Sisters heard Edith tell the Germans that she was still
waiting for a passport. "The street was crowded with

people protesting this outrage.... At the street corner the Gestapo van waited for them."

That evening, the newspaper carried an article by the German Kommissar-General: Because the Dutch hierarchy had refused to "respect the confidential nature of these negotiations," the German authorities were to "consider Jewish Catholics as their worst enemies" and "see to it that they be deported with all dispatch to the east."

Two police vans, one carrying thirteen prisoners, the other seventeen—including the Stein sisters—arrived at Amersfoort at 3 in the morning. The prisoners were beaten with cudgels and cast into a hut without being fed.

On August 5, a telegram came to the Carmel from the town of Westerbork, in northern Holland. It requested clothing, blankets and medicines for the Stein sisters. The sisters of Echt sent these by way of messengers, including in the packet a holy card on which Edith had written her wish to sacrifice her life for the conversion of the Jewish people.

The young men sent from the convent to bring these items saw Edith at the camp. While telling them what had happened since they had left the convent, "she was calm and serene.... Her eyes shone with the mysterious radiance of saintliness. Quietly and soberly, she described everything that had happened to those around her, but never mentioned her own troubles. She especially wanted the sisters to be told that she still was wearing her religious habit and that it was her intention and the intention of all the other religious (there were about ten of them) to keep on wearing their habits until the end. She described the joy of the other prisoners in learning that priests and sisters were among them. They became the one hope and support to these poor people, who were expecting the very worst at any time. She was glad to give her fellow-prisoners any consolation by word and prayer. Her deep faith created an atmosphere of grace and peace around her. Several times she insisted that we reassure the Reverend Mother and the sisters.... She prayed almost all day long, except when she had to get her food. She never spoke one word of complaint."[14]

At the Westerbork camp, Edith met her friend Ruth Kantorowicz, who had been taken from the Ursuline convent in Venloo. A messenger sent from Venloo to bring something to Ruth saw Edith with her. Edith told him, "Whatever happens, I am prepared. The Child Jesus is with us even here."

Two survivors of the frightful odyssey brought back the account of what happened to her there, and we fully reproduce it here. A Jewish businessman testifies: "Sister Benedicta stood out from among those brought to the prison camp (Westerbork) on the fifth of August, because of her great calm and recollection. The cries, distress and confused state of the new arrivals was indescribable. Sister Benedicta went among the women as an angel of mercy, calming and helping them. Many of the mothers were on the verge of madness, succumbing to a black and brooding melancholy. They neglected their children and could only weep in dumb despair. Sister Benedicta took care of the little children, washing them, combing their hair, bringing them food, and looking after their other basic needs."

Another eyewitness writes: "Edith's silence distinguished her from the other religious. She seemed to me to be suffering immensely, but peacefully. I can't express it any better than by saying that she seemed to carry such suffering on her shoulders that even her smile languished. She rarely spoke and often cast inexpressibly sad glances at her sister Rosa.... She thought about the trials she had foreseen—not her trials, but those of the others." The glances she gave Rosa show us how she suffered for others, but she continually prayed and filled her soul with peace.

On August 6, she managed to get a few lines through to the prioress, telling of the departure of the first convoy for Silesia or Czechoslovakia. For Rosa, she requested wool stockings, blankets, woolen underclothing, a crucifix, and a rosary. For herself, she requested the next volume of the breviary and their identification cards. She added: "So far, prayer has been coming along *marvelously.*"

On August 7, one of Edith's former pupils, standing on the platform of the Schifferstadt railroad station, heard Edith call out from the train, "Greet the sisters of St. Magdalena for me. I am headed east."

Another message to the prioress—undated—contained just a few lines: "Under the present circumstances, it is better I try nothing more.[15] In any event, I commit myself entirely into Your Reverence's hands and whatever you decide to do. *I am quite content now. One can only learn the* Scientia Crucis *if one truly suffers under the weight of the Cross. I was entirely convinced of this from the very first and I have said with all my heart: Hail, Cross, our only hope.*"

On February 16, 1950, the *Official Journal* of Holland published the following lines in a list of the victims of deportation:

> No. 44074—Edith—Teresa—Hedwig—STEIN—born 12 October, 1891, in Breslau—arrived from Echt—died 9 August, 1943 [typographical error; it should have read 1942, and the same for Rosa, whose date the *Official Journal* gave as 4 May, 1950:]

> No. 44075—Rosa—Maria—Agnes—Adelaid STEIN— born 13 December, 1883, at Lublintz (Ger.)—arrived from Echt—died 9 August, 1942.

We know nothing more about them except that they were killed at Auschwitz.

The Carmelites of Cologne announced Sister Benedicta's death and concluded with:

"We shall look for her here on earth no longer, for she has been called to God, who accepted her sacrifice, which will bear much fruit in the people for whom she prayed, suffered and died."

Chapter 9

The Message of Edith Stein

What is a conversion? The word itself means "a turning toward." For the religious, the Catholic, conversion is a turning toward the Love which is the creative act of the entire universe, expressed at every moment in keeping the universe and all creatures in the state of being. Love-made-man, who takes upon himself all the evil in humanity, is the Sustainer of the universe. He gave himself up freely to be crucified, so that he could use absolute evil as an instrument to save the world.

To convert to Catholicism is to understand the beginning and the end of every created being. It is to live one's whole life in trying to better understand this. It is the turning of one's whole being to the Light which illuminates the mind and to the All-Powerful One who brought the world into existence.

No one was more thoroughly *converted* than Edith Stein.

If life is so profoundly meaningful, then no conversion is more significant for our age than hers.

Because her intellect caught sight of the total necessity, Edith began to take her first shaky steps on the road to the faith. She took them out of rational necessity. Edith was not led by the sentiment of her heart, and her motives were not properly religious ones.

From the very beginning, Edith Stein probed deeply into the mystery of the world and was not satisfied with merely examining the surface appearance of things and the universe. She was a wholly logical woman. She was one who from the outset—like her whole epoch, but with more insight, more complete exigency—rejected an idealism in which the post-Cartesian mind only toyed with superficial ideas of reality. Her mind had to examine the whole complexity of existence, for she saw that if it did not, it would only waste itself in useless and dishonorable sport.

But, at this stage in her progression, Edith perceived, along with Max Scheler and others, that one cannot enter into the very heart of things, one cannot enter into being, without *sympathy*, without participation and communion. Here, she desired to grasp the world by fully understanding it; she wanted to enter into existence *with* others, in the fellowship of destinies which do not have their full existence, which only come to fully know themselves as beings if each projects on the other the "image" of a love that becomes knowledge because it is participation in a birth in being.

And here, we must recognize that Edith Stein is in some way the answer to a shallow existentialism. It is true that, if we do not welcome others in existence with love, we reduce them to nothingness, we *annihilate* them, while reducing our own selves to nothingness. Then, it is only too true that "hell is others." There is no being without love. Love is like the interior light of the world. If it disappears, all that *could be* is reduced to the nothingness of darkness. But with an act of love, all comes into being.

Now God made this act of love by the perpetual rebirth which is creation, and by sharing his loving act with each member of creation. Golgotha bore witness to the perfection of his creative love. When Edith turned herself entirely toward the universal Being, she could not avoid encountering the Crucified's act of love—and she encountered him.

She experienced this love because she met some men and women who lived it and, in living it, brought life.

She encountered it and *prolonged* it until she offered herself for "her people."

Some have rightly said that Edith Stein's life is more important than what she wrote. To be exact, whatever she wrote only has full meaning in the light of what she was.

In *turning toward* Christ, she turned herself toward the most traditional philosophy of the Church, thomism. We can argue about how she sometimes used thomistic thought. But the important thing is that she knew how to advance by the strength of her whole being, by the meaning of her entire life. She came to see that to understand the universe one had to come to see that it demanded the light of love and that the light of love gave the intellect much more in return.

"The love of God," writes Rousselot, "will always be more noble than the knowledge of God.... But submission, the proper act of love, will tend toward intellectualism. The act of being completely united, will be to know."[1] Edith Stein, a marvelous example of a Christian philosopher, constantly reached for this rigorous knowledge, strengthened in her journey by the lessons of exactitude she had learned in her youth.

Being and knowing are one and the same God. We struggle along the path of knowledge and love like poor, exhausted travelers, and the path is that wonderful reconciliation of the faculties of being, something hard for us to perceive. And, failing to grasp at the same time the two ends of the chain, we rush headlong into the insane illusion of understanding without loving and into the disheartening resignation of loving without understanding. We are tossed about from pride to despair, finding repose only in a despair proud in resignation.

Edith Stein understood: "I find myself constantly on the verge of annihilation and I must receive being at every instant." To this truth, Edith dedicated the certainty of her death, offered and consented to. The most desperate of existentialisms says what Edith said. But she went on to say that it suffices for one ounce of love and *sacrifice* to secure access to the infinite kingdom of being which is not given in exchange, but freely offered.

The very *certitude* of Edith on the road to Auschwitz—"I am quite content now"—is the only response to the existential *anxiety*. No one can deny the infinite reality of this anxiety. It is in every one of us, lurking in the heart of a mystic, and in the soul of everything that exists: our being is not *ours*, it is parceled out one instant at a time. An expression of hatred or omission can throw us out of being and into nothingness.

But the world is there to teach us its lesson. The slow plodding of human reason up the ladder of creation tells us that *all things have meaning*, provided we look upon the world with love.

Edith Stein was beatified in Cologne by Pope John Paul II on May 1, 1987. Perhaps one day the Church will canonize her. For us, she is already the patroness of the unity of knowledge and love. Edith told her despairing era that it was right in despairing, because it had separated knowledge from love, taking the road of denial: but there is another path. We have only to turn our gaze, as she did.

The Jewish religion taught Edith the way to love, by instilling in her the desire for exactitude. This book bears witness to a love that came to know the Beloved through respect for knowledge.

Notes

Chapter 1

1. Also called the Day of Reconciliation.
2. Franz Rosenzweig, *L'Anné Juive*.
3. Sr. Aldegonde Jaegerschmidt, OSB. Radio message on the tenth anniversary of Edith Stein's death, Stuttgart, 1952. Cf. Sr. Teresia de Spiritu Sancto, OCD, *Edith Stein*, trans. Hastings and Nicholl, Sheed and Ward, 1952.
4. Sr. Aldegonde Jaegerschmidt, OSB.
5. Difficult to translate. Possibly something like "the troop of poets" or "the poets corner."
6. Cf. Hilda C. Graef, *The Scholar and the Cross*, Newman Press, 1955.
7. Cf. Sr. Teresia de Spiritu Sancto, op. cit.
8. Ibid.

Chapter 2

1. B. Fondane, *La Conscience Malheureuse*.
2. Edmund Husserl, *Logical Investigations*.
3. Edmund Husserl, *Cartesian Meditations*.
4. Ibid.
5. We shall not go into its implications or values.
6. *Compte Rendu des Journées de Juvisy: "La Phénoménologie,"* Editions du Cerf.
7. Edmund Husserl, *Formal and Transcendental Logic*.
8. In philosophy only. He had come quite close to Christ before his death.
9. Jacques Maritain, *The Degrees of Knowledge*.
10. J.M. Oesterreicher, *Sept Philosophes Juifs Devant le Christ*, Editions du Cerf.
11. Later, a professor at the Sorbonne.
12. Scheler ultimately left the Church.

Chapter 3

1. Edith found literally tens of thousands of shorthand notes waiting for her. These are now preserved in the Husserl Archives at Louvain—Tr.

2. J.M. Oesterreicher, op. cit.

3. *Beiträge zur Philosophischen Begründung der Psychologie, Jahrbuch,* 1922, Vol. 5.

4. Cf. *L'Introduction à la Philosophie,* or *Situation Spirituelle de Notre Époque.*

5. C G Jung, *Psychology and Religion.*

6. Cf. "Letters of Frau Conrad-Martius" in *Edith Stein.*

7. That Edith Stein wrote this text during this particular period is verified by a well-informed witness, Marie Biemas *Katolische Frauenbildung,* November, 1952.

8. Henri Bergson, *Two Sources of Morality and Religion.*

9. Frau Conrad-Martius thought that Edith Stein assisted at Mass daily from that very night of her encounter with St. Teresa. Edith also accompanied Frau Martius to the Temple.

10. In the private chapel of the Bishop of Speyer.

Chapter 4

1. Edith observed the Jewish fasts.

2. Edith herself used these terms.

Chapter 5

1. Testimony of a Dominican religious from Speyer, in *The Scholar and the Cross.*

2. Collected in French under the heading *La Femme et Sa Destinée,* Amoit-Dumont, Publishers.

3. Edith Stein, *La Femme et Sa Destinée,* p. 107.

Chapter 6

1. Sr. Aldegonde Jaegerschmidt, who knew Edith during her school days, later became a convert from Protestantism and entered the Benedictine convent of St. Lioba at Freiburg, which Edith visited several times.

2. Testimony by Dom Walzer, Abbot of Beuron. Cf. Sr. Teresia de Spiritu Sancto, op. cit., Part II, Chapter II.

3. Sr. Teresia de Spiritu Sancto, op. cit., p. 114.

4. Cf. *L'Introduction à la Philosophie,* or *Situation Spirituelle De Notre Époque.*

Chapter 7

1. *Endliches und Ewiges Sein*, Freiburg-Louvain, 1950.
2. Let us keep in mind that here we are presenting only the barest outline of a highly intricate thought.

Chapter 8

1. Author of *The Eternal Woman*, *The Song at the Scaffold* (which inspired Bernanos to write his *Dialogues Des Carmelites*) and many other fine books.
2. Sr. Teresia de Spiritu Sancto, op. cit., cf. p. 181.
3. Ibid., cf. Part II, Chapter III.
4. *Kreuzwissenschaft*, Louvain-Freiburg, 1950. We readily see the six years of crucifixion reflected in the spiritual experience that united Edith to her master in spirituality.
5. We shall not go into discussions regarding Edith Stein's definition of faith. Hilda C. Graef is evidently correct in preferring the definition of the Epistle to the Hebrews to that of Edith. Cf. *The Scholar and the Cross*.
6. *The Prayer of the Church*. This translation is made from the French text of the *Editions de l'Orante*—Tr.
7. Edith did not mean this to be interpreted as the singular function of the community Office, which expresses the Church.
8. *La Prière de l'Eglise*, Paderborn, 1936.
9. Ibid.
10. At the time of the voting, the prioress thought it advisable for Edith to vote without divulging her origins.
11. Bismarck's long struggle against Catholicism.
12. She completed *The Science of the Cross*.
13. Verses 13 and 14.
14. Account written by the young men sent from the convent to the sisters.
15. Meaning to escape or be allowed to get safely to Switzerland. They both hoped for Switzerland until the last moment.

Chapter 9

1. Rousselot, *The Intellectualism of St. Thomas*.

St. Paul Book & Media Centers

ALASKA
750 West 5th Ave., Anchorage, AK 99501 907-272-8183.

CALIFORNIA
3908 Sepulveda Blvd., Culver City, CA 90230 310-397-8676.
1570 Fifth Ave. (at Cedar Street), San Diego, CA 92101 619-232-1442;
   619-232-1443.
46 Geary Street, San Francisco, CA 94108 415-781-5180.

FLORIDA
145 S.W. 107th Ave., Miami, FL 33174 305-559-6715; 305-559-6716.

HAWAII
1143 Bishop Street, Honolulu, HI 96813 808-521-2731.

ILLINOIS
172 North Michigan Ave., Chicago, IL 60601 312-346-4228; 312-346-3240.

LOUISIANA
4403 Veterans Memorial Blvd., Metairie, LA 70006 504-887-7631;
   504-887-0113.

MASSACHUSETTS
50 St. Paul's Ave., Jamaica Plain, Boston, MA 02130 617-522-8911.
Rte. 1, 885 Providence Hwy., Dedham, MA 02026 617-326-5385.

MISSOURI
9804 Watson Rd., St. Louis, MO 63126 314-965-3512; 314-965-3571.

NEW JERSEY
561 U.S. Route 1, Wick Plaza, Edison, NJ 08817 908-572-1200.

NEW YORK
150 East 52nd Street, New York, NY 10022 212-754-1110.
78 Fort Place, Staten Island, NY 10301 718-447-5071; 718-447-5086.

OHIO
2105 Ontario Street (at Prospect Ave.), Cleveland, OH 44115 216-621-9427.

PENNSYLVANIA
214 W. DeKalb Pike, King of Prussia, PA 19406 215-337-1882; 215-337-2077.

SOUTH CAROLINA
243 King Street, Charleston, SC 29401 803-577-0175.

TEXAS
114 Main Plaza, San Antonio, TX 78205 210-224-8101.

VIRGINIA
1025 King Street, Alexandria, VA 22314 703-549-3806.

CANADA
3022 Dufferin Street, Toronto, Ontario, Canada M6B 3T5 416-781-9131.